The Random House DINOSAUR TRAVEL GUIDE

BY KELLY MILNER HALLS

COME SEE THE
AMAZING GIA...

Greetings...

Dinosaurs 37

ILLUSTRATIONS
BY LUIS V. REY

RANDOM HOUSE
NEW YORK

SEND MORE TOURISTS!

S0-EAW-832

To my favorite dinosaur—my father, Gene Milner; to the memory of my mom, Georgia Milner; to my grandmother, Thelma Lea Ketchum, who walked along dinosaur tracks as a young girl more than eighty years ago; and, as always, to my daughters, Kerry and Vanessa, who remind me there is promise in the future as well as in the past.

Literally hundreds of interviews with people in the United States and Canada went into making this book as complete and as accurate as possible. It would take pages to list all the science and museum experts who contributed their time and knowledge, and there would be a danger of leaving a few out if I even made that attempt. So please accept this blanket acknowledgment as genuine appreciation on my part to anyone and everyone who responded to my research. I am grateful beyond measure.

The author and editor would like to thank Dr. Matt Lamanna, Assistant Curator of Vertebrate Paleontology at the Carnegie Museum of Natural History, for his assistance in the preparation of this book.

Cover photograph copyright © John-Marshall Mantel/CORBIS
Cover map copyright © MAPS.com/CORBIS
Cover footprints and "stamp" illustrations copyright © Luis V. Rey

www.randomhouse.com/kids

Educators and librarians, for a variety of teaching tools, visit us at www.randomhouse.com/teachers

Library of Congress Cataloging-in-Publication Data
Halls, Kelly Milner.
The Random House dinosaur travel guide / by Kelly Milner Halls. — 1st ed.
p. cm.
ISBN 0-375-82715-3 (trade pbk.)
1. Dinosaurs—United States—Guidebooks—Juvenile literature.
2. United States—Guidebooks. I. Title.
QE861.5.H34 2005
567.9'0973—dc22
2004004740

Printed in the United States of America
10 9 8 7 6 5 4 3 2 1
First Edition

CONTENTS

INTRODUCTION

One of the greatest mysteries on Earth unfolded 65 million years ago. Dinosaurs—tiny to towering—that had once thrived on every continent on the planet sadly slipped into extinction. But after they died, they left behind thousands of fossilized clues.

As modern-day dinosaur detectives called paleontologists sift through the rock and soil we now call the United States of America, they hear prehistoric whispering. With wonder and respect, they carefully piece together the skeletons of dinosaurs, marine reptiles, flying reptiles, and mammals. And as the puzzle pieces come together, so do the real-life stories that go with them.

This book is called a travel guide, but it's much more than a directory of fossil exhibits across North America. It is a guide to sharing in those bone diggers' discoveries as you journey across this once-prehistoric land. It's a road map to the past, for those of us trapped in the present. It gives us all a chance to literally look back in time.

So grab your sneakers and indulge your passion for paleo. It's time to hit the dinosaur trail!

Astrodon

Utahraptors

HOW TO USE THIS BOOK

IT'S ALL IN THE DETAILS . . .

In my last dinosaur travel guide, *Dino-Trekking,* I included fees, contact information, and details about accessibility. Like prehistoric animals, those fees and facts evolved as the years passed, making the book out-of-date.

It's impossible to prevent evolution, of course. Nor would we want to! So in this updated volume, I've omitted some of the changeable details, like fees and disability-friendly features. The best way to gather the most current facts about those details is to use the contact information I have provided—addresses, phone numbers, e-mail addresses, and Web sites—and to ask about them.

Of course, addresses and phone numbers and so on are also subject to change—and I apologize in advance for the changes that will no doubt occur between revisions of this book. (A hint: If you find a Web site is no longer live on the Internet, look for the name of the exhibit host using your favorite search engine. If the host still exists, odds are good it will have a new and improved Web site.)

Each state-specific chapter includes a "Bone Digger Bonus," a special feature highlighting an exhibit or fossil find within that state or region. Some of paleontology's most amazing experts have shared their insights for these articles, so be sure to take a look. You'll also find contact information at the end of each chapter for the region's geological survey office. Those regional geologists may have even more fossil information available, so be sure to contact them before your next dinosaur road trip.

—K.M.H.

*Tyrannosaurus rex
and Anatotitan*

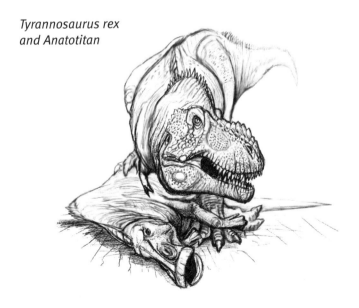

ANNISTON MUSEUM OF NATURAL HISTORY

Created in 1930, when Pennsylvania businessman H. Severn Regar moved to Anniston and donated his collection of natural history specimens to the city, the Anniston Museum of Natural History is one of the largest of its kind in the modern Southeast. Expect to see a pterosaur with a wingspan of 30 feet and a 3-ton *Albertosaurus*, colored to reflect the theory of dinosaurs' evolutionary ties to modern birds.

> 800 Museum Dr.
> Anniston, AL 36207
> (256) 237-6766
> Web site: http://www.annistonmuseum.org
> E-mail: info@annistonmuseum.org

McWANE CENTER

While the McWane Center has tons of great science on display, its Greene County mosasaur is the crown jewel of a fairly substantial fossil collection. This remarkable prehistoric marine reptile is reconstructed and on display, complete, in a beautiful case.

> 200 Nineteenth St. N.
> Birmingham, AL 35203
> (205) 714-8300
> Web site: http://www.mcwane.org
> E-mail: form on Web site

MANN WILDLIFE LEARNING MUSEUM AT THE MONTGOMERY ZOO

Adjacent to the Montgomery Zoo, this wildlife learning center is primarily an exercise in taxidermy, with exhibits of more contemporary animal reconstructions. But a small fossil collection, including saber-toothed cats, prehistoric wolves, and woolly mammoths, offers a glimpse of Alabama's prehistoric past.

> 315 E. Vandiver Blvd.
> PO Box 3242
> Montgomery, AL 36110
> (334) 240-4900
> Web site: http://www.mannmuseum.com
> E-mail: mannmuseum@mindspring.com

BONE DIGGER BONUS

DINOSAURS OF ALABAMA

Interview with Dr. David T. King, Jr.
Professor of Geology at Auburn University
http://www.auburn.edu/~kingdat

Author's Note: If you're in search of the king of Alabama dinosaurs, geology professor Dr. David T. King, Jr., of Auburn University is the man you need to see. For more than two decades, Dr. King has made and studied discoveries that help define Alabama's unique prehistory, including the state's most complete tyrannosaur and the massive Wetumpka meteor crater.

Are there dinosaur fossils in Alabama?

> Dr. King: *Yes. I'm not sure when the first dinosaur was found in Alabama, but the 1940 Field Museum of Chicago expedition to the dinosaur quarry at Harrell's Station in Dallas County more or less put Alabama "on the map" of places to look for dinosaur fossils. There are twenty-one known specimens of dinosaurs from Alabama. Many of these are a single bone or tooth.*

Why are dinosaur fossils somewhat rare in Alabama?

> Dr. King: *Alabama dinosaurs, like most eastern dinosaurs, are found in marine sediments where they washed offshore. The land where they lived was often too acidic for bones, teeth, or eggshells to be fossilized here.*

What other prehistoric fossils are common in Alabama?

> Dr. King: *Other Cretaceous reptiles found include pterosaurs, birds, turtles, pliosaurs, and mosasaurs. In rocks younger than Cretaceous, there are many prehistoric fossils, including our state fossil, the Eocene whale, and mastodon teeth. In older rocks, we have tracks of large prehistoric reptiles and amphibians. In the coal-mining areas, there are large tree, fern, and other plant fossils.*

Can you describe your most exciting Alabama fossil discovery?

> Dr. King: *This [particular] dinosaur discovery was quite unexpected. It was made after a new road was cut through a small hill made of chalk. The road-building equipment cut through the skeleton, which was about 40 percent complete. It took several years to extract all the bones from the small hill, which had to be cut down. It is a juvenile dinosaur akin to the* Albertosaurus, *but [it] is older than the* Albertosaurus *of Canada.*

Albertosaurus

11

ALABAMA MUSEUM OF NATURAL HISTORY

During the Coal Age, 300 million years ago, ancient Walker County, Alabama, looked nothing like the landscape we see today. The murky swamplands were home to strange creatures like the four-toed amphibian or reptile *Cincosaurus*. Its tracks and other fossils are on display in this museum, along with a ferocious reptile of the prehistoric ocean, *Mosasaurus*. Several mosasaur skeletons are being prepared for display, along with other fossil specimens from the region.

University of Alabama

Smith Hall

Box 870340

Tuscaloosa, AL 35487

(205) 348-7550

Web site: http://www.museums.ua.edu/history

E-mail: programs@bama.ua.edu

GEOLOGICAL SURVEY OF ALABAMA
420 HACKBERRY LN.
TUSCALOOSA, AL 35486
(205) 349-2852
WEB SITE: HTTP://WWW.GSA.STATE.AL.US
E-MAIL: INFO@GSA.STATE.AL.US

ALASKA

ALASKA MUSEUM OF NATURAL HISTORY

Operated until 1999 by an all-volunteer staff, this relatively new and growing museum features an exhibit called Alaska Dinosaurs and Marine Reptiles—a four-part presentation of geological maps, facts and fallacies, a panorama, and the state's largest collection of regional prehistoric fossils, including the partial skeleton of "Lizzie"—a hadrosaur and Alaska's oldest known dinosaur.

201 N. Bragaw St.
Anchorage, AK 99508
(907) 274-2400
Web site: http://www.alaskamuseum.org
E-mail: webcontact@alaskamuseum.org

DENALI NATIONAL PARK AND PRESERVE

According to collections manager Dana Woodard, the Denali National Park visitors center has "a collection here on loan from a gentleman named James Kunkle, who collected ivory carvings from all over the state. Included in this collection are a mammoth tusk, two mastodon tusks, and a mammoth tooth. In another collection of ivory carvings donated to us is a single mammoth tusk."

PO Box 9
Denali Park, AK 99755
(907) 683-2294
Web site: http://www.nps.gov/dena
E-mail: form on Web site

BONE DIGGER BONUS

THE EYES HAVE IT: ARCTIC EXTRAS

Did the dinosaurs of Alaska have any special Arctic "extras" to help them survive? According to a December 19, 2000, article in the Dallas Morning News *and a feature in the* Journal of Vertebrate Paleontology, *the answer may be yes. Reporter Alexandra Witze interviewed Alaska paleontologist Dr. Roland Gangloff about the meat-eating* Troodon, *whose teeth have been found scattered across acres and acres of Alaska's North Slope.*

According to Witze, Troodon *teeth are rare in the lower forty-eight states, and yet dozens and dozens have been found in Alaska. Why? Evolution, say Dr. Gangloff and his research partner, Dallas paleontologist Anthony Fiorillo of the Dallas Museum of Natural History.* Troodon *evolved giant eyes to improve its low-light vision, and so it achieved hunting success during the long, dark Alaskan nights. Witze reports that a typical bipedal meat-eater of* Troodon's *size had a skull with eye sockets less than an inch in diameter.* Troodon, *in contrast, had 2-inch eye sockets. Bigger eyes—better night vision. Not all paleontologists agree with the wide-eyed theory. How will this mystery unfold? We'll just have to wait and see.*

Troodon

13

ARIZONA

MUSEUM OF NORTHERN ARIZONA

Hard to imagine, but the San Francisco Peaks in the bustling city of Flagstaff are actually the remains of an enormous dormant prehistoric volcano! The Museum of Northern Arizona's geology gallery examines the evidence in paleontological detail, including a life-size skeletal model of *Dilophosaurus,* a carnivorous dinosaur found nearby.

> 3101 N. Fort Valley Rd.
> Flagstaff, AZ 86001
> (928) 774-5213
> Web site: http://www.musnaz.org
> E-mail: info@mna.mus.az.us

MESA SOUTHWEST MUSEUM

Perhaps best known for its Southwest Paleontology Club and Southwest Paleontological Symposiums, this (literally) *growing* museum has a remarkable collection of dinosaur exhibits and specimens. Animated dinosaurs and articulated fossil skeletons (including *Tyrannosaurus rex*) inhabit the museum, and with its recently completed expansion, the Mesa Southwest Museum contains one of the largest exhibitions of dinosaurs west of the Mississippi River. Featured are new exhibits showcasing Arizona's underwater past and bizarre "sea monsters" of the Jurassic Period of the Mesozoic Era.

> 53 N. McDonald Dr.
> Mesa, AZ 85201
> (480) 644-2230
> Web site: http://www.cityofmesa.org/swmuseum
> E-mail: swmuseum.info@cityofmesa.org

Zuniceratops

BONE DIGGER BONUS

HE'S NOT "KIDDING" AROUND

By the time Chris Wolfe was six, he was pretty handy around a dinosaur dig site. He knew to look for rocklike pieces that were darker than the ordinary minerals scattered across the Arizona badlands. His father, Douglas—a Mesa Southwest Museum paleontologist—had explained that those dark pieces could be dinosaur fossils, so Chris kept his eyes peeled.

His eagle-eyed determination paid off big-time in the fall of 1996 (at the age of eight) when he discovered Zuniceratops christopheri, *a new Cretaceous dinosaur 90 million years old. Just half an hour after this particular adventure had begun, Chris found the horn tip of the dinosaur. His discovery led to the excavation of three* Zuniceratops, *a hadrosaur, a raptor-like carnivore, and more.*

"It was great," Chris remembers. "When you find something, everyone gets so excited."

According to the New Mexico Museum of Natural History curator, Spencer Lucas, there was good cause for excitement: "Nobody had ever found this kind of horned dinosaur in rock this old in North America. Chris's discovery pushed the fossil record of these kinds of horned dinosaurs further back in time."

GRAND CANYON CAVERNS

From 1957 to 1962, these remarkable natural formations were called the Dinosaur Caverns. Today they're known as the Grand Canyon Caverns (though they are more than 120 miles from the Grand Canyon), but a friendly 20-foot-tall *T. rex* reminds visitors of their proud history. Sculpted of sheet metal and concrete, it's not scientifically accurate, but it's a fun photo op, and the caverns are out of this world. Don't miss the sad mummified bobcat preserved within the caverns.

> (Hist. Rte. 66, 22 miles west of Seligman)
> PO Box 180
> Peach Springs, AZ 86434
> (928) 422-3223
> Web site: http://www.gccaverns.com
> E-mail: info@gccaverns.com

PETRIFIED FOREST NATIONAL PARK

Around 225 million years ago, crocodile-like prehistoric reptiles; giant, fish-eating amphibians; and small dinosaurs roamed the land that would one day be called Arizona. Today their fossilized remains and simulated skeletal models haunt the terrain (and visitors center), along with thousands of petrified pieces of *Araucarioxylon arizonicum*, *Woodworthia*, and *Schilderia* trees. Once collected without caution, this stonelike ancient wood cannot legally be removed from the park. Similar samples from private property can be purchased nearby.

PO Box 2217

Petrified Forest National Park, AZ 86028

(928) 524-6228

Web site: http://www.nps.gov/pefo

E-mail: form on Web site

RAINBOW FOREST MUSEUM

The Petrified Forest National Park hosts Junior Ranger adventures with the help of the staff and resources of the Rainbow Forest Museum, located at the south entrance of the national park. Exhibits include early reptiles, dinosaurs, and petrified wood common to the area, plus a collection of petrified wood returned by guilty tourists—complete with letters of apology!

Petrified Forest National Park

PO Box 2217

Petrified Forest National Park, AZ 86028

(928) 524-6228

Web site: http://www.nps.gov/pefo

E-mail: form on Web site

ARIZONA SCIENCE CENTER

Only two permanent casts of Mesozoic reptiles are on display at the Arizona Science Center's World Around You gallery—a *T. rex* skull and a full cast of an *Anhanguera*. (The *Triceratops* skull is apparently in storage.) But traveling dinosaur exhibits, like Dragon Bones: When Dinosaurs Ruled China, are regularly booked at the center, so check for details before you visit.

600 E. Washington St.

Phoenix, AZ 85004

(602) 716-2000

Web site: http://www.azscience.org

E-mail: info@azscience.org

ROBERT S. DIETZ MUSEUM OF GEOLOGY

Arizona is a haven for fossil hunters. And the Robert S. Dietz Museum of Geology on the Arizona State University campus is a haven for the ancient fossils they find. Curator Brad Archer oversees a carnivorous *Smilodon fatalis*—a saber-toothed cat that lived 10,000 to 50,000 years ago; a 50-foot-long prehistoric shark (*Carcharocles megalodon* of the Miocene-Pliocene Epoch); the Chandler mammoth (*Mammuthus columbi*); and a *Triceratops horridus*, or "terrifying three-horned face," found in South Dakota.

Physical Sciences Complex, F-Wing

Box 871404

Arizona State University

Tempe, AZ 85287

(480) 965-7065

Web site: http://geology.asu.edu/resources/museum

E-mail: b.archer@asu.edu (Brad Archer, curator)

ARIZONA-SONORA DESERT MUSEUM

Local geology student Rich Thompson first discovered *Sonorasaurus*—the 20-ton brachiosaur star of the Arizona-Sonora Desert Museum's Ancient Arizona exhibit—in 1994 as he searched for petrified wood chips. Embedded in sandstone, Thompson knew this fossil was no petrified piece of wood. It turned out to be a saurian pelvis—a very *large* pelvis! Thompson's dig-site discovery zone was carefully duplicated for this (2000) museum exhibit.

2021 N. Kinney Rd.

Tucson, AZ 85743

(520) 883-2702

Web site: http://www.desertmuseum.org

E-mail: info@desertmuseum.org

ARIZONA GEOLOGICAL SURVEY
416 W. CONGRESS, STE. 100
TUCSON, AZ 85701
(520) 770-3500
WEB SITE: HTTP://WWW.AZGS.AZ.GOV
E-MAIL: TOM.MCGARVIN@AZGS.AZ.GOV (GEOLOGIST)

Smilodon

ARKANSAS

MID-AMERICA SCIENCE MUSEUM

Trackways cast from those discovered in Nashville, Arkansas, are on display at this generalized, hands-on science museum. Not a lot for dinophiles, but according to locals, other fun stuff will dazzle you.

500 Mid-America Blvd.

Hot Springs National Park, AR 71913

(800) 632-0583

(501) 767-3461

Web site: http://www.midamericamuseum.org

E-mail: NA

MUSEUM OF DISCOVERY

Fossils aren't regularly on display, but traveling exhibits do occasionally visit the Museum of Discovery. Call in advance to find out. The museum features a yearly fund-raiser called the Dino Dash—a fun run with prizes for the most creative dinosaur costumes. Before-and-after activities test your dino-knowledge and skills. The Dino Dash is usually held at the end of May.

500 President Clinton Ave., Ste. 150

Little Rock, AR 72201

(800) 880-6475

(501) 396-7050

Web site: http://www.amod.org

E-mail: mod@amod.org

VARDELLE PARHAM GEOLOGY CENTER

This educational facility provides hands-on geology workshops for students throughout the state. One of the most popular classes is on fossil preparation. It is one of the only authentic dinosaur destinations in Arkansas, because so little dinosaur fossil information has been unearthed in the state. (Although *Ornithomimus*-like tracks and fossil traces have been discovered in Nashville and Little Rock, Arkansas.)

3815 W. Roosevelt Rd.

Little Rock, AR 72204

(501) 296-1877

Web site: http://www.state.ar.us/agc/agc.htm

E-mail: agc@arkansas.gov

Ornithomimid

MOUNTAINBERG CITY PARK DINOSAURS

You won't find mineralized fossils here. These dinosaurs were made of concrete over thirty years ago so local children would have something fun to climb. Not serious science, but a great photo op if you're traveling nearby.

U.S. Hwy. 71, near Mountainberg City Hall

NASHVILLE, ARKANSAS

Even the community logo of Nashville is built around a dinosaur, because dinosaur tracks found all over the town are its most amazing claim to fame.

Web site: http://www.nashvillearkansas.com

ARKANSAS GEOLOGICAL COMMISSION
VARDELLE PARHAM GEOLOGY CENTER
3815 W. ROOSEVELT RD.
LITTLE ROCK, AR 72204
(501) 296-1877
WEB SITE: HTTP://WWW.STATE.AR.US/AGC
E-MAIL: AGC@ARKANSAS.GOV

BONE DIGGER BONUS

ARKANSAS FARMER'S DINOSAUR FIND

Like so many mysteries, there's not much to go on when it comes to "Arkansaurus fridayi"— the only dinosaur fossil ever unearthed in the state of Arkansas. These fossilized foot bones are the only scraps of proof that dinosaurs once ran across the prehistoric landscape (aside from dozens of dinosaur tracks).

Farmer J. B. Friday unearthed the fossils near Lockesburg in Sevier County in 1972 while searching for a wandering cow. He donated them to scientists at the University of Arkansas. Experts who studied the discovery revisited the dig site in hopes of finding more of the mysterious biped, but with only an additional toe bone found, they were mostly unsuccessful.

Even so, experts from the Arkansas Geological Commission believe the fossil foot belonged to an ornithomimid-like dinosaur and informally named it for farmer Friday. Little else is known about this particular dinosaur. Where are the rest of its remains? It's almost anyone's guess. One theory says the rare bones were ground into gravel and used to help build Arkansas Highway 24. So when you roll past Lockesburg, Arkansas, toot your horn for "Arkansaurus fridayi."

DISNEYLAND

In the 1960s, Disneyland opened Primeval World, a diorama of "typical" dinosaur life, as imagined in that decade. First displayed as a part of the 1964 World's Fair, the exhibits took up residence on the Disneyland Railroad ride between Tomorrowland and Main Street. Obviously, they represent another era in dinosaur theory, but that can be interesting to see with current science in mind. You'll also catch some dinosaur glimpses on the Big Thunder Railroad, including fabricated dinosaur bones and lush tropical greenery that looks as if it belongs in a prehistoric world.

>1313 S. Harbor Blvd.
>
>Anaheim, CA 92803
>
>(714) 781-4565
>
>Web site: http://www.disneyland.com
>
>E-mail: NA

UNIVERSITY OF CALIFORNIA MUSEUM OF PALEONTOLOGY

One of the most extensive fossil collections on Earth is held in trust by the University of California Museum of Paleontology. As a result, much more is carefully stored away than is on display. But that allows for frequent special exhibits, as well as old favorites from the permanent collection. Everything from traditional dinosaur favorites like *T. rex* and *Triceratops* to *Parasaurolophus* to prehistoric turtles and flying reptiles are part of the expe-

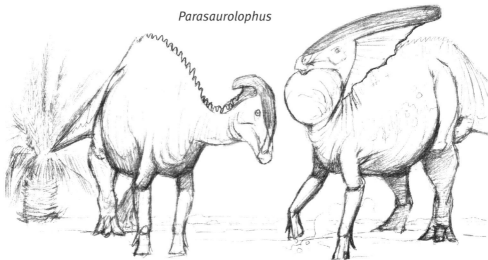

Parasaurolophus

rience. And dozens of guest speakers stop by to lecture at the university museum. So be sure to schedule your visit around one of those special discussions.

1101 Valley Life Sciences Bldg.

Berkeley, CA 94720

(510) 642-1821

Web site: http://www.ucmp.berkeley.edu

E-mail: ucmpwebmaster@uclink.berkeley.edu

ANZA-BORREGO DESERT STATE PARK

You won't immediately see any fossil evidence as you stroll into this California state park. You'll only recognize a bit of the paleo-past if you're an expert—or visit with one. But experts know that within these 600,000 acres are fossils up to 4.5 million years old, from marine invertebrates (like clams and shells) to prehistoric mammals from four different time periods. The park also features wildlife, including the endangered peninsular bighorn sheep— for which the park was named. (The Spanish word *borrego* refers to bighorn sheep.) Ask about the Leapin' Lizards activity offered by the visitors center— a look at the thriving reptiles that inhabit the landscape today.

200 Palm Canyon Dr.

Borrego Springs, CA 92004

(760) 767-5311

Web site: http://www.anzaborrego.statepark.org

E-mail: NA

DINOSAURS OF CABAZON

Many things have changed since these dinosaur monuments were con-structed of concrete (1,200 bags!) and scavenged steel bridge parts in 1964. The restaurant that was the *T. rex* and *Apatosaurus*'s original companion has been replaced by fast-food stops. Various forms of fencing have come and gone—replaced, for the time being, by a grassy stretch fit for a paleo-picnic. Some say even the dinosaurs' quirky charm has faded. But you can still buy cheap trinkets from the gift shop located in the belly of the long-necked dino (featured in *Pee-Wee's Big Adventure*). Not to be missed by die-hard dinophiles!

Rte. I-10 (north side)

Cabazon, CA 92230

(951) 922-8700 (gift shop)

Web site: NA

E-mail: NA

THE PETRIFIED FOREST

One of the finest examples of a fossilized Pliocene forest in the world, this family-run attraction was started by a man known as "Petrified Forest Charlie." Notable visitors have included paleontologist O. C. Marsh, who in 1870 came to see the stone wood and took back some samples to study, and author Robert Louis Stevenson, who wrote about the trees after a visit to the unique forest. Today, the Hawthorne family tries to fill Charlie's adventurous boots. You can buy tiny samples of petrified wood, as well as other mineral treasures, in the gift shop.

4100 Petrified Forest Rd.

Calistoga, CA 94515

(707) 942-6667

Web site: http://www.petrifiedforest.org

E-mail: manager@petrifiedforest.org

NORTHERN CALIFORNIA NATURAL HISTORY MUSEUM

Although the Northern California Natural History Museum—a collaborative effort between the California State University at Chico and the College of Natural History—has not opened as of 2006, the dream is still alive. An annual golf tournament, a lecture series called the Northern California Natural History Museum Without Walls, and other efforts continue to move the city of Chico closer to permanently housing its collection of fossil resources from the state's rich mammalian and marine prehistoric history. Contact the museum's executive director, Greg Liggett, for up-to-the-minute information on the NCNHM's progress.

California State University

Chico, CA 95929

(530) 898-4121

Web site: http://www.ncnhm.org

E-mail: gliggett@ncnhm.org (Greg Liggett, executive director)

RAYMOND M. ALF MUSEUM OF PALEONTOLOGY

In 1937, math and science teacher Dr. Raymond M. Alf took his students at the Webb School of California into the desert in search of fossils. There they discovered a new species of prehistoric pig, or peccary, and a love of paleontology. A lifetime later, the educational museum—the only one of its kind on a high school campus—was founded to serve the community and inspire a passion for science among students. More than 95 percent of the museum's 70,000 fossils were discovered and prepared by students. It was granted accreditation by the American Association of Museums in 1998. The Hall of Life and the Hall of Footprints include many, *many* fascinating displays.

1175 W. Baseline Rd.
Claremont, CA 91711
(909) 624-2798
Web site: http://www.alfmuseum.org
E-mail: hmoffat@webb.org

CHAPMAN'S GEM AND MINERAL MUSEUM

Teacher recommended, this obscure museum has over 3,000 square feet of gems, minerals, and fossils on display. Also exhibited are Native American artifacts from the Fortuna region. A great gift shop gives you the chance to buy local fossils for your collection.

(4 miles south of Fortuna on Hwy. 101)
PO Box 852
Fortuna, CA 95540
(707) 725-4732
Web site: NA
E-mail: NA

NATURAL HISTORY MUSEUM OF LOS ANGELES COUNTY

In addition to one of the best-preserved *Tyrannosaurus rex* skulls in the country, the Natural History Museum of Los Angeles County has one of the richest collections of prehistoric fossil fish, sharks, and marine reptiles in the world, second only to the Smithsonian Institution in Washington, DC! The Page Museum—poised on the edge of the legendary La Brea Tar Pits—rounds out the museum experience with some of the most amazing fossilized prehistoric mammals in the world. The combination of the two facilities makes this a once-in-a-lifetime paleo-stop *not* to be missed.

900 Exposition Blvd.
Los Angeles, CA 90007
(213) 763-3466
Web site: http://www.nhm.org
E-mail: info@nhm.org

OAKLAND MUSEUM OF CALIFORNIA

Nestled in Oakland, across the bay from San Francisco, you'll find this multi-purpose museum. And within its exhibits, you'll find the exciting Rustler Ranch Mastodon Project—on the discovery, preparation, and display of a nearly complete prehistoric mastodon. Ranch hand Eric Pedersen stumbled across this prehistoric elephant-like creature in 1997 while hard at work at the

Rustler Ranch. At first, only a tooth was visible from the stream bank. But ranch owner Roger Fiddler was intrigued and called in a paleontologist to identify the fossil. As the team unearthed the mastodon, they discovered it was complete (except for its tusks), and in the same position as it was when it died. You can explore the Rustler Ranch mastodon for yourself, if you visit this urban museum.

1000 Oak St.

Oakland, CA 94607

(510) 238-2200

Web site: http://www.museumca.org

E-mail: webmaster@museumca.org

SAN BERNARDINO COUNTY MUSEUM

Robust describes the exhibits and the impressive general 200,000-specimen collection in the paleontology section of the San Bernardino County Museum's Geological Science exhibit. Three staff members carefully present many of those fossils, most collected during their own fieldwork nearby. One of the most notable recent finds was evidence of the largest prehistoric bird ever to walk what we now call California: a partial humerus, or wing bone, of the extinct *Aiolornis incredibilis* ("incredible bird god of the winds"), which lived 2 million years ago near Murrieta, in Riverside County, California. Senior field paleontologist for the San Bernardino County Museum, Quintin Lake, found the specimen. It was officially described by Kathleen B. Springer, senior curator of geological science at the museum.

2024 Orange Tree Ln.

Redlands, CA 92374

(909) 307-2669

Web site: http://www.co.san-bernardino.ca.us/museum

E-mail: museum@sbcounty.gov

SAN DIEGO MUSEUM OF MAN

Four million years of human evolution are beautifully described and exhibited at the San Diego Museum of Man—thanks to a grant from the National Science Foundation. The $2 million, 7,000-square-foot hands-on exhibit is separated into five galleries. Each was "designed to engage visitors and help them start thinking about age-old questions, including time, genetics, and the environment," says the museum's director of development, Melinda Newsome, on the museum's Web site. "The exhibit is unique, in that guests are invited to touch nearly all of its contents."

1350 El Prado, Balboa Park
San Diego, CA 92101
(619) 239-2001
Web site: http://www.museumofman.org
E-mail: khamilton@museumofman.org (Kathleen Hamilton,
    curator of education)

BONE DIGGER BONUS

GIANT FOSSIL BIRD FOUND IN MURRIETA

(Courtesy of the San Bernardino County Museum)

A partial humerus, or wing bone, of an extinct Incredible Teratorn, the largest bird of flight ever identified in North America, has been discovered by San Bernardino County Museum paleontologists from 2-million-year-old deposits near Murrieta, in Riverside County, California. The find has resulted in a new name for the extinct avian giant: Aiolornis incredibilis *("incredible bird god of the winds"). The discovery was made by Quintin Lake, senior field paleontologist for the San Bernardino County Museum.*

Teratorns were the largest known flying birds. Teratorns living in South America during the Miocene Epoch—about 5 to 8 million years ago—reached a wingspan of 6 to 8 meters (up to 26 feet) and weighed from 72 to 79 kilograms (159 to 174 pounds). The fossil from Murrieta suggests a wingspan of up to 5.5 meters (18 feet). A few scattered and fragmentary fossils of the Incredible Teratorn have also been discovered in Nevada and in the Anza-Borrego Desert in San Diego County. The Murrieta specimen is the most anatomically distinctive of these fossils, and analysis of this bone prompted a new name for the extinct predator.

"Quintin's find is the icing on the cake for us," says Kathleen B. Springer, senior curator of geological sciences. "For years the museum has searched extensively in the rocks in and around the Murrieta area looking for fossil treasures. The giant teratorn is just one of thousands of fossils curated and housed at the SBCM from this region. It proves again that if you look in the right places, rocks can reveal abundant and exciting new information about past life." Eric Scott, curator of paleontology, adds, "Fossils of large animals from Murrieta are usually from extinct mammals—mammoths, mastodons, ground sloths, large horses, and other animals of that size. Birds are very rare because their bones are thin and fragile and don't often preserve well. Quintin's fossil is most unusual in that context. We're glad he has such good eyes!"

SAN DIEGO NATURAL HISTORY MUSEUM

Dinosaur fossil finds are rare in California. But San Diego Natural History Museum paleontologist Brad Riney made one of those discoveries (bits and pieces of a hadrosaur in the sea cliffs of La Jolla) in 1967 when he was just in junior high school! More hadrosaur fossils were collected in 1986 and 1989 from the Carlsbad Research Center. And in 1987, a partial skeleton of a nodosaur was discovered, preserved after it washed out to sea and settled on the ocean floor. These remarkable finds make the San Diego Natural History Museum a great place to visit on the dinosaur trail.

1788 El Prado, Balboa Park

PO Box 121390

San Diego, CA 92112

(619) 232-3821

Web site: http://www.sdnhm.org

E-mail: webteam@sdnhm.org

CALIFORNIA ACADEMY OF SCIENCES

Before the California Academy of Sciences temporarily moved to 875 Howard Street (also in San Francisco) to make room for renovations at the homesite, it hosted a nice cross section of dinosaur material, including a stunning *Tyrannosaurus rex* skeletal mount and exhibit, Life Through Time: Evidence for Evolution. Paleo resources are in storage until the museum update is complete in 2008. But even the smaller, short-term location will host temporary dinosaur exhibits, so check with the staff for details. And be sure to consider visiting after 2008, when the museum will reinstall its dinosaurs and a new rain forest habitat, along with other surprises.

California Academy of Sciences

(temporary address)

875 Howard St.

San Francisco, CA 94103

(permanent address after renovations)

55 Concourse Dr.

Golden Gate Park

San Francisco, CA 94118

(415) 321-8000

Web site: http://www.calacademy.org

E-mail: info@calacademy.org

Imagine a mammoth—a great prehistoric elephant—lumbering across the plains of an ancient world. Now picture it the size of a pony. That's precisely what paleontologist Dr. Larry Agenbroad and his field team found in August 1994 on Santa Rosa Island, off the shore of Santa Barbara. One of the most complete specimens of a pygmy mammoth (*Mammuthus exilis*) ever excavated, it is now proudly studied and displayed at the Santa Barbara Museum of Natural History. Other fossils common to prehistoric California are also on display, but this stunning mammoth is the star of the collection.

2559 Puesta del Sol Rd.

Santa Barbara, CA 93105

(805) 682-4711

Web site: http://www.sbnature.org

E-mail: info@sbnature2.org

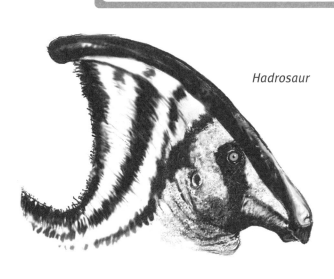

CALIFORNIA GEOLOGICAL SURVEY
HEADQUARTERS/OFFICE OF THE STATE GEOLOGIST
801 K ST., MS 12-30
SACRAMENTO, CA 95814
(916) 445-1825
WEB SITE: HTTP://WWW.CONSRV.CA.GOV/CGS
E-MAIL: CGSHQ@CONSRV.CA.GOV

Hadrosaur

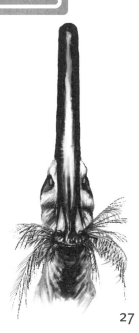

UNIVERSITY OF COLORADO MUSEUM

Standing beside the *Triceratops* skull on display at the University of Colorado Museum is a humbling experience. It's so massive, it dwarfs the people who admire it. It's well worth seeing, along with the literally thousands of other fossils within the extensive collection. But one of the museum's greatest assets is its vertebrate paleontology curator, Dr. Karen Chin. Dr. Chin is the undisputed queen of coprolites—aka fossil poop. So having her on staff at the museum is like housing a dinosaur celebrity. She's following in some big footsteps. Dr. Robert T. Bakker was associated with the museum for years.

UCB 218

University of Colorado

Boulder, CO 80309

(303) 492-6892

Web site: http://cumuseum.colorado.edu

E-mail: cumuseum@colorado.edu

THE DINOSAUR DEPOT MUSEUM

Decades of dinosaur history are alive and well at the Dinosaur Depot in Cañon City. Legendary bone hunters, including Edward Drinker Cope, Othniel Charles Marsh, John Bell Hatcher, and many others, made regular stops in this Colorado region to collect fossils for museums out of state. When the Garden Park Paleontology Society finally raised enough money to keep a few of the bones at home, the Dinosaur Depot was born in a restored turn-of-the-century firehouse. A replica of one of the finest *Stegosaurus* specimens ever collected is on display, as is the only fossilized Jurassic tree ever unearthed in the area. And you'll love the welcoming committee—a collection of dinosaur skulls!

The Garden Park Paleontological Society

330 Royal Gorge Blvd.

Cañon City, CO 81212

(719) 269-7150

Web site: http//www.dinosaurdepot.com

E-mail: webmaster@dinosaurdepot.com

DENVER MUSEUM OF NATURE AND SCIENCE

Formerly the Denver Museum of Natural History, the museum changed its name and logo in May 2000 to better express its broad commitment to both nature and science education. But the exceptional $7.7 million Prehistoric Journeys exhibit remains unaltered. More than 17,000 square feet of space allows the museum's visitors to walk through the 3.5-billion-year history of life on Earth, which includes an impressive array of dinosaur skeletal mounts. Expect to see *T. rex, Stegosaurus, Allosaurus, Diplodocus, Coelophysis,* and much, *much* more.

> 2001 Colorado Blvd.
> Denver, CO 80205
> (800) 925-2250
> (303) 322-7009
> Web site: http://www.dmnh.org
> E-mail: feedback@dmns.org

DICK'S ROCK MUSEUM

Looking for a family-run business for Colorado fossil fun? Put Dick's Rock Museum at the top of your list. Dick Siebenaler moved to Colorado from Nebraska with his wife, Marilyn, on a whim in 1964 and turned the Estes Park rock shop into an urban legend. Fossils are not only on display—they are for sale, along with other terrific rocks and minerals.

> 490 Moraine Ave.
> Estes Park, CO 80517
> (970) 586-4180
> Web site: NA
> E-mail: NA

Stegosaurus

WATERWORLD

WaterWorld claims to be one of the biggest water parks in North America, boasting 30 acres of wet-and-wild warm-weather fun. But it's the theme park–style Journey to the Center of the Earth attraction, not the comparative splash value, that makes WaterWorld rank among the destinations of dino-cooldom. Thousands of adventurous visitors each year make their way past the turnstiles, into four-person floats, and through a "crack" in the Earth's crust in search of $2.2 million worth of dinosaur thrills. "We wanted to create something unique," says park spokesman Rick Fuller. "And most people agree, Journey to the Center of the Earth is a one-of-a-kind experience." More than a dozen lifelike animated models of dinosaurs (including *Tyrannosaurus rex* and *Triceratops*) and other prehistoric creatures (water-bound plesiosaurs and flying pterosaurs) roar and ramble throughout the five-minute excursion.

> 1800 W. Eighty-ninth Ave.
> Federal Heights, CO 80260
> (303) 427-7873
> Web site: http://www.waterworldcolorado.com
> E-mail: guestservices@hylandhills.org

FLORISSANT FOSSIL BEDS NATIONAL MONUMENT

Between 60,000 and 80,000 Late Eocene fossil specimens, nearly 35 million years old, have been recovered from Colorado's remarkable Florissant Fossil Beds National Monument in the last hundred years. Some of the best samples are on display at the park's visitors center. Outside the center is a marked interpretive trail featuring enormous petrified tree stumps preserved by a volcanic eruption. This is a terrific opportunity to discover prehistoric plant life on the fossil trail.

> 15807 Teller County 1
> PO Box 185
> Florissant, CO 80816
> (719) 748-3253
> Web site: http://www.nps.gov/flfo
> E-mail: form on Web site

DINOSAUR JOURNEY MUSEUM

Located just outside Grand Junction, the Dinosaur Journey Museum (part of the Museum of Western Colorado) houses a dozen or more life-size, animated dinosaur dioramas, along with interactive, hands-on educational exhibits for kids. A state-of-the-art working fossil lab adds real science to the electronic dinosaur fun. DinoDigs offers families the chance to dig for real dinosaur bones from the rugged Colorado landscape during the summer field season as well. It's a must for any dinosaur traveler in western Colorado.

550 Jurassic Ct.
Fruita, CO 81521
(888) 488-3466
(970) 858-7282
Web site: http://www.dinosaurjourney.org
E-mail: jfoster@westcomuseum.org

THE MUSEUM OF WESTERN COLORADO

The blending of Grand Junction's robust dinosaur resources into one *mega*-travel destination was a streamlined stroke of genius that put the region's treasures under the same "roof." The museum itself is a terrific local museum with paleontological and other exhibits unique to western Colorado.

BONE DIGGER BONUS

FLORISSANT FOSSIL BEDS NATIONAL MONUMENT

When you roll into Florissant, Colorado, the word fossil *creeps into your field of vision again and again and again. It seems the whole town is proud of the prehistoric discoveries made in and around Teller County during the last hundred years.*

According to park ranger Tom Ulrich, 60,000 to 80,000 Late Eocene fossil specimens, nearly 35 million years old, have been recovered from Florissant Fossil Beds National Monument. And while most have been distributed to educational facilities around the world, several hundred of the best fossils are on exhibit at the park's visitors center.

"After a traumatic volcanic eruption," says Ulrich, "feather-light ash settled on bits of plants, seeds, leaves, and insects, creating a very gentle form of preservation. Every minute detail was captured. As a result, Florissant Fossil Beds National Monument is known primarily for the incredible detail and diversity of our plant and insect fossils."

Dozens of petrified sequoia tree stumps just outside the visitors center are as massive as the plant and insect specimens inside are delicate. "Again, these are volcanic fossils," says Ulrich. "Silica-rich mudflow preserved these stumps." The mineral-rich waters saturated the massive tree trunks, eventually replacing the organic matter with a mineralized, or petrified, mirror image. The protective coating of volcanic ash and river sediments protected the ancient fossils underground until scientists discovered and excavated them millions of years later.

"We estimate there are eighty to one hundred stumps preserved at Florissant Fossil Beds National Monument," says Ulrich, "but less than half are exposed." Once a fossil is exposed to natural elements of erosion like weather, it is in danger. Leaving the fossils underground is the best way to protect them.

But once you're at the museum's main headquarters in downtown Grand Junction, you'll be poised to sign up for everything paleo the community has to offer, including Dinosaur Journey; the family DinoDig; and three historic working dig sites with marked trails—Riggs Hill, Dinosaur Hill, and the Rabbit Valley Research Natural Area.

462 Ute Ave.

Grand Junction, CO 81501

(970) 242-0971

Web site: http://www.wcmuseum.org

E-mail: kfiegel@westcomuseum.org

DINOSAUR TRAILS OF PURGATOIRE VALLEY

Considered one of the most magnificent sauropod trackways in the United States, this paleo-treasure can only be experienced in the company of an expert National Park Service guide. The tracks were long overlooked after their discovery in 1935 because they are so difficult to access—more than 16 miles of very rugged trail must be hiked just to capture a glimpse. But these days die-hard and *fit* fossil fans make the journey with expert help on a regular basis. Be sure to contact NPS trail expert Gary Weiner in Denver at gary_weiner@nps.gov or (303) 969-2855 for more information. This hike is absolutely *not* for beginners.

1420 East Third St.

La Junta, CO 80150

(719) 384-2181

Web site: NA

E-mail: NA

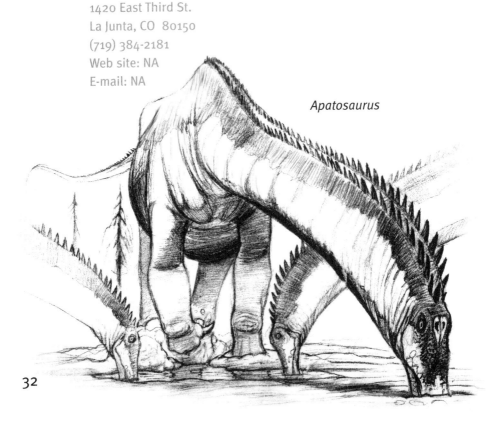

Apatosaurus

MORRISON NATURAL HISTORY MUSEUM/DINOSAUR RIDGE

If you were just passing by, you might never notice the fossil treasure of Dinosaur Ridge. At first glance, it looks like a thousand other roadside landscapes in a thousand other towns. But on this steep, rocky hillside, dinosaurs like *Apatosaurus* and *Iguanodon* left their footprints behind millions of years ago as they walked along a prehistoric beach. It is one of the most amazing dinosaur stops I've ever had the chance to explore—a stop no dinophile should miss. The visitors center offers a number of guided and self-guided tour options. And while you're in Morrison, visit Dinosaur Ridge's sister museum, the Morrison Natural History Museum (501 Colorado Hwy. 8) for a rustic, hometown look at some of the dinosaur fossils found nearby, including a *T. rex* skull.

> The Friends of Dinosaur Ridge Visitors Center
>
> 16831 W. Alameda Pkwy.
>
> Morrison, CO 80465
>
> (303) 697-3466
>
> Web site: http://www.dinoridge.org
>
> E-mail: tours@dinoridge.org

ROCKY MOUNTAIN DINOSAUR RESOURCE CENTER

There are dozens of exhibits at this wonderful new 18,000-square-foot museum located roughly 30 miles from Denver. One of the most amazing is "the world's smallest *T. rex*"—a baby *Tyrannosaurus rex* nicknamed "Sir William." Many prominent dinosaur experts regularly lecture here, and the gift shop is full of exceptional paleo-materials. It's a great stop and a great addition to the Colorado dinosaur community.

> 201 S. Fairview St.
>
> Woodland Park, CO 80863
>
> (719) 686-1820
>
> Web site: http://www.rmdrc.com
>
> E-mail: info@rmdrc.com

COLORADO DIVISION OF MINERALS AND GEOLOGY
1313 SHERMAN ST., RM. 215
DENVER, CO 80203
(303) 866-3567
WEB SITE: HTTP://WWW.MINING.STATE.CO.US

CONNECTICUT

PEABODY MUSEUM OF NATURAL HISTORY AT YALE UNIVERSITY

One of the Peabody's most famous paleo-assets is the remarkable (but out-dated) mural by artist Rudolph Zallinger, *The Age of Reptiles*. Overlooking the Great Hall in Yale's Peabody Museum, it is a reminder of the past that (starting in 1943) took four and a half years to complete. Beyond the mural are 55,000 cataloged specimens, many of which date back to the classic Bone Wars between Yale's Othniel Charles Marsh and Philadelphia's Edward Drinker Cope. Dozens of respected paleontologists have followed in Marsh's footsteps to help the collection grow.

> 170 Whitney Ave.
> New Haven, CT 06520
> (203) 432-5050
> Web site: http://www.peabody.yale.edu
> E-mail: peabody.webmaster@yale.edu

DINOSAUR STATE PARK

Dinosaur State Park opened in 1968, two years after thousands of dinosaur tracks were unearthed during the excavation of a proposed state building site. Five hundred of the 2,000 tracks are now protected and preserved beneath the exhibit center's geodesic dome. What happened to the other 1,500? They were reburied for preservation. These tracks, of the footprint genus called *"Eubrontes"* by specialists in dinosaur prints, were probably made by *Dilophosaurus*. Bring your own bucket, cooking oil, plaster of Paris, and rags or paper towels, and park officials will help you make a dinosaur-track cast of your own.

> 400 West St.
> Rocky Hill, CT 06067
> (860) 257-7601 (Friends of Dinosaur Park and Arboretum)
> (860) 529-8423 (Park)
> Web site: http://www.dinosaurstatepark.org
> E-mail: questions@dinosaurstatepark.org

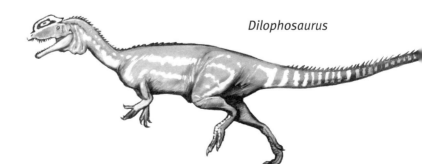

Dilophosaurus

BONE DIGGER BONUS

DR. JOHN H. OSTROM

Retired Curator, Peabody Museum of Natural History at Yale University

Author's Note: Dr. Ostrom discovered and named Deinonychus, *one of the most ferocious and most fascinating meat-eating "raptors," in the summer of 1964 and turned paleontology's thoughts on dinosaurs upside down. This is his report, in his own words, on what it was like to find such a memorable fossil. Dr. Ostrom died in July 2005.*

The day of the discovery, I left our field camp at Cashen Ranch on the Crow Indian Reservation in Montana and set out in our field vehicle with my assistant, Grant Meyer. Our objective was to check out and assess a dozen new sites. By noontime, I was disappointed because none of them seemed very promising, and I had decided not to excavate any of them [the] next year.

After driving for more than forty-five minutes, we reached a very colorful butte isolated from the main Cloverly outcrop and started walking along its north slope. Grant was about one pace ahead of me, when I saw an unbelievable object about 10 feet in front of him: a very distinctive claw, just lying on the slope. I bumped against Grant as I dashed by him, almost knocking him down the slope. He laughed at me, but by then he'd seen why I was in such a rush.

We knelt side by side, looking at that beautiful claw—almost perfectly preserved. Then we began to see bone fragments nearby, and then more fragments scattered down the slope. Then, just a couple of inches from the first claw, I saw a less obvious, much smaller claw of a different shape. I had never seen anything like this before. Was it part of a skeleton?

I told myself, "Don't touch anything. Photograph the site first. Then scour the area to gather every fragment." Only then did Grant and I hunker down and slowly, very delicately, begin probing the weathered surface in the hopes that more, unweathered bones remained. The rest—what followed from our discovery on the last day of the 1964 field season (August 29, 1964)—is history.

There is the moment, just as I remember it. I knew at once that our find was brand-new—as it proved to be—and so, so very different.

CONNECTICUT GEOLOGICAL AND NATURAL HISTORY SURVEY

THE DEPARTMENT OF ENVIRONMENTAL PROTECTION

79 ELM ST.

HARTFORD, CT 06106

(860) 424-3000

WEB SITE: HTTP://DEP.STATE.CT.US/CGNHS

E-MAIL: DEP.WEBMASTER@PO.STATE.CT.US

DELAWARE MUSEUM OF NATURAL HISTORY

Famous for ornithology, this teaching museum also has two Chinese dinosaurs on exhibit. *Tuojiangosaurus*, a plant-eating stegosaur, had more plates and spikes than its North American cousin, *Stegosaurus*. And *Yangchuanosaurus*, a ferocious carnivore, was related to *Allosaurus*.

4840 Kennett Pike
PO Box 3937
Wilmington, DE 19807
(302) 658-9111
Web site: http://www.delmnh.org
E-mail: NA

THE DELAWARE VALLEY PALEONTOLOGICAL SOCIETY

For a fee, you can join the Delaware Valley Paleontological Society (which is actually headquartered in neighboring New Jersey) and receive its monthly newsletter and yearly scientific journal, *The Mosasaur*. The field trips you'll learn about and fossil friendships you'll make are more than worth the investment if you're in the Delaware/New Jersey region, aching to sock away a little active dig time.

c/o Stephen Kurth
37D Monroe Path
Maple Shade, NJ 08052
Web site: http://www.dvps.org
E-mail: NA

DELAWARE GEOLOGICAL SURVEY
UNIVERSITY OF DELAWARE
NEWARK, DE 19716
(302) 831-2833
WEB SITE: HTTP://WWW.UDEL.EDU/DGS
E-MAIL: DELGEOSURVEY@UDEL.EDU

BONE DIGGER BONUS

U-PICK FOSSILS

Hooray! The Delaware Geological Survey, together with the U.S. Army Corps of Engineers, offers amateur fossil fans the chance to collect tiny marine specimens from locations that were vast prehistoric seas during the Cretaceous Period. According to the DGS, the Chesapeake and Delaware Canal near the Reedy Point Bridge foundation is one of the best places to find the official state fossil, Belemnitella americana, *an ancient squidlike animal. Rumor is, at least three duckbill teeth, a duckbill vertebra, and several toe bones from a theropod have also been found in the canal spoils. South of Dagsboro on Route 113 and Pepper Creek, there are Pleistocene plant fossils. And the Coursey and Killen Ponds near Felton have also yielded Miocene fossils. Write to the DGS for "Special Publication Number 21" for more information about these fossil locations.*

Cryolophosaurus

DISTRICT OF COLUMBIA

SMITHSONIAN NATIONAL MUSEUM OF NATURAL HISTORY

Museums under the Smithsonian banner are world famous for their exhibits, and the National Museum of Natural History is no exception. Expect to see some of the finest fossil resources in the world, including many fully mounted skeletal reconstructions.

Tenth St. and Constitution Ave. NW
Washington, DC 20560
(202) 633-1000
Web site: http://www.mnh.si.edu
E-mail: info@si.edu

THE GEOLOGICAL SOCIETY OF WASHINGTON

Founded in 1893, this gathering of geology buffs is only partially dedicated to paleontology and fossils. But when they meet every month at the John Wesley Powell Auditorium (2170 Florida Ave. NW, Washington, DC), they are following in a proud tradition more than 110 years old. E-mail J. A. Speer for details on membership fees and requirements as well as for information about upcoming events.

3635 Concorde Pkwy., Ste. 500
Chantilly, VA 20151
(703) 652-9950
Web site: http://www.gswweb.org
E-mail: j_a_speer@minsocam.org

BONE DIGGER BONUS

CALLED TO DIG: DR. MICHAEL BRETT-SURMAN

Before Dr. Michael Brett-Surman joined the staff of the National Museum of Natural History, he was a kid like everyone else. And while he was amazed by the T. rex *he saw as a kid at the American Museum of Natural History in New York City—"One look," he says, "and I was hypnotized"—it wasn't until college that he realized dinosaurs would become his life's work. Brett-Surman knew he wanted to work in a museum, but as he studied the history of Earth, he found that "the further back in time, the more interesting things got."*

Fossil hunter Barnum Brown, who helped collect the American Museum's astonishing dinosaur specimens, was just one of his personal heroes. But as the years have passed, Brett-Surman has earned a reputation of his own, teaching field courses, writing papers and books, and helping to care for one of the world's most extensive fossil collections.

Barnum Brown

BREVARD MUSEUM OF HISTORY AND SCIENCE

This small museum is dedicated to exploring the natural resources of Brevard County and the rest of east-central Florida. Dinosaurs were not a natural part of Florida's prehistory, so expect exhibits on ancient mammals and sea creatures, including a display called Tooth and Claw, a fossil exhibit with descriptions offered—even in Braille. Guided nature walks (reservations required) and the children's Discovery Room round out the fun.

2201 Michigan Ave.

Cocoa, FL 32926

(321) 632-1830

Web site: http://www.brevardmuseum.org

E-mail: bmhs@brevardmuseum.org

GRAVES MUSEUM OF ARCHAEOLOGY AND NATURAL HISTORY

When "Uncovering the past, one layer at a time" is your museum slogan, you can be pretty sure people will expect paleontology exhibits. This community-friendly museum doesn't disappoint. A cast of Stan's—the Black Hills Institute's second-most-famous *T. rex*'s—skull is on display, along with other prehistoric fish, mollusk fossils, and prehistoric mammals. The museum's Adventure Team hosts regular family fossil field trips to Peace River in search of Ice Age animal fossils. Look for great exhibits on prehistoric people as well.

481 S. Federal Hwy.

Dania Beach, FL 33004

(954) 925-7770

Web site: http://www.gravesmuseum.org

E-mail: education@gravesmuseum.org

MUSEUM OF ARTS AND SCIENCES

Florida's lengthy fossil record is beautifully exhibited at the museum's Center for Florida History. Featured is a 13-foot-tall ground sloth (*Eremotherium laurillardi*) unearthed in the 1970s. The living creature weighed 3 to 5 tons and gobbled 300 pounds of plant matter each day. Also on display is one of the best specimens of *Cuvieronius,* an ancient elephant relative that roamed Pleistocene Florida along with the sloth 130,000 years ago. Fifty-one other mammals were also discovered in the rich Daytona Bone Beds with these two amazing individuals.

352 S. Nova Rd.
Daytona Beach, FL 32114
(386) 255-0285
Web site: http://www.moas.org
E-mail: NA

THE GILLESPIE MUSEUM OF MINERALS AT STETSON UNIVERSITY

It's not the most impressive museum in the state, but a small cross section of index fossils, ammonites, brachiopods, trilobites, fossil crabs, ferns, and other prehistoric representations, along with a modest collection of dinosaur goods—a dinosaur track, agatized dinosaur bones, and other mineralized specimens—make it a nice stop if you're in the area.

234 E. Michigan Ave.
DeLand, FL 32723
(386) 822-7330
Web site: http://www.gillespiemuseum.stetson.edu
E-mail: hvanater@stetson.edu

FLORIDA MUSEUM OF NATURAL HISTORY

Florida's geologic history is robust but young when compared to the day of the dinosaur. So the Florida Museum of Natural History has a remarkable collection of prehistoric fossils and exhibits not related to dinosaurs. Consider, for example, the popular exhibit called Tusks! Ice Age Mammoths and Mastodons, which explores the largest collection of Florida's prehistoric elephants ever assembled in one exhibit space. Expect to learn a great deal about ancient marine life and more recent extinct mammals—all a rich part of Florida's paleo-past.

University of Florida Cultural Plaza
SW Thirty-fourth St. and Hull Rd.
PO Box 112710
Gainesville, FL 32611
(352) 846-2000
Web site: http://www.flmnh.ufl.edu
E-mail: frontdsk@flmnh.ufl.edu

MUSEUM OF SCIENCE AND HISTORY

Prehistoric Park at the MOSH (Museum Of Science and History) is one of the most popular stops. Their cherished *Allosaurus* skeleton recently got a well-deserved makeover, and the hands-on fossil displays have been renovated as well, to include fossils and informational markers that bring prehistory into focus.

1025 Museum Circle
Jacksonville, FL 32207
(904) 396-6674
Web site: http://www.themosh.org
E-mail: webmaster@themosh.org

Allosaurus

BONE DIGGER BONUS

EXOTIC UNDERWATER FLORIDA

by Russ McCarty
Florida Museum of Natural History

Florida is an exotic place. In the Late Paleozoic Era, the major continents of the world were one supercontinent, now called Pangaea. Sometime around the Early Jurassic, the continents we know today began to break apart from Pangaea. Florida—originally part of the African plate—was left behind as part of North America. For the next 140 million years, Florida was underwater.

Although dinosaurs never lived in Florida, when it comes to fossils from the Age of Mammals, Florida is probably the richest state east of the Mississippi. The oldest surface rocks are about 50 million years old and contain mainly invertebrate fossils that lived in these ancient Florida seas. One occasionally finds vertebrate fossils in the limestone— bones and teeth from sharks, bony fish, whales, dolphins, walruses, and sea cows.

Between 24 million and 5 million years ago, in the Miocene Epoch, land animals occupied most of present-day Florida. Animals from this period include three-toed horses, primitive cats, hyena-like dogs, giant bear-dogs (Amphicyon), rhinos, gomphotheres (elephant relatives), camels, alligators, crocodiles, tortoises, peccaries, otters, and many strange-looking antelope-like animals.

Miocene fossil-collecting sites are fairly common in Florida. The most famous area is the phosphate-mining region east of Tampa. Miners have found so many bones in their search for phosphate that they named the area Bone Valley; geologists later renamed it the Bone Valley Formation. Limestone quarries often contain Miocene fossils. Shark teeth are common, including those of Carcharocles megalodon, the extinct 60-foot-long shark, which had teeth 8 inches long.

41

WALT DISNEY WORLD

Once you step into DinoLand USA, you'll see dinosaur data near and far. Consider the Cretaceous Trail, a peaceful path lined by plants and animals that once shared Earth with the dinosaurs; the Boneyard, a simulated dig site where kids can play in the dirt with simulated dinosaur bones; the Primeval Whirl, a kickin' roller coaster that drops you into the jaws of a simulated dinosaur; the TriceraTop Spin, a whirling, playful ride with a secret for small children; and Dinosaur, a thrill ride that takes you back in time.

Disney's Animal Kingdom/DinoLand USA

7521 W. Irlo Bronson Mem. Hwy.

Kissimmee, FL 34747

(407) 939-6244

Web site: http://disneyworld.disney.go.com/wdw/index

E-mail: form on Web site

MULBERRY PHOSPHATE FOSSIL MUSEUM

Mining for phosphate—a mineral used in soaps and other products—stirred up some interesting by-products: prehistoric fossils. This small museum, housed in a turn-of-the-century train depot, explores the secrets left behind in the phosphate deposits of Florida.

Hwy. 37 S.

PO Box 707

Mulberry, FL 33860

(813) 425-2823

Web site: NA

E-mail: NA

UNIVERSAL STUDIOS ORLANDO

Thanks to the wonders of *Jurassic Park*, Universal Studios Orlando has become a dinosaur treasure in Florida. The Jurassic Park River Adventure ride sends you floating—no, make that *splashing*—through a prehistoric lagoon gone wrong and straight into a *T. rex*'s mouth! The Jurassic Park Discovery Center blends real dinosaur science with the imaginative wonders of the blockbuster films, from dinosaur hatchlings to fossil remains. Camp Jurassic is a playground of dinosaurian proportions. Pteranodon Flyers offer high-flying transportation across the park. And finally, the Triceratops Discovery Trail brings these robotic dinosaurs to life before your very eyes. A great dinosaur adventure, by any standard.

1000 Universal Studios Plaza
Orlando, FL 32819
(407) 363-8000
Web site: http://www.universalorlando.com
E-mail: NA

DINOSAUR WORLD

Heralded by the Florida press as the "world's largest dinosaur attraction,"
Dinosaur World (near Tampa) is a stellar dinosaur stop, featuring more than a
hundred fleshed-out dinosaur models in parklike tropical outdoor settings,
an extensive gift shop, and a picnic area/playground. For a complete list (and
photos) of each dinosaur model, see the user-friendly Web site.

5145 Harvey Tew Rd.
Plant City, FL 33565
(813) 717-9865
Web site: http://www.dinoworld.net
E-mail: florida@dinoworld.net

MUSEUM OF FLORIDA HISTORY

Many exhibits that reveal Florida's state history are on display at this extensive museum. Also on display is a 12-foot-tall mastodon, as well as other prehistoric mammal and marine fossil resources common to the state.

500 S. Bronough St.
Tallahassee, FL 32399
(850) 245-6400
Web site: http://dhr.dos.state.fl.us/museum
E-mail: form on Web site

FLORIDA GEOLOGICAL SURVEY
GUNTER BLDG., MS #720
903 W. TENNESSEE ST.
TALLAHASSEE, FL 32304
(850) 488-4191
WEB SITE: HTTP://WWW.DEP.STATE.FL.US/GEOLOGY
E-MAIL: FORM ON WEB SITE

GEORGIA MUSEUM OF NATURAL HISTORY

A beautiful but slightly complex Web site makes it clear this natural history museum has much more than fossils available for exploration. But the paleontology collection includes more than 1,200 fossils and casts of prehistoric life—including Paleozoic fossils—from southeastern locations in and near Georgia. It's a nice stop in a college town known for activity and fun.

Natural History Bldg.
University of Georgia
Athens, GA 30602
(706) 542-1663
Web site: http://museum.nhm.uga.edu
E-mail: musinfo@uga.edu

FERNBANK MUSEUM OF NATURAL HISTORY

Fernbank is a remarkably beautiful natural history museum. Add two of the most amazing giants in dinosaur history and you have a travel stop well worth exploring when you're in or near Atlanta. Thanks to the magic of Dinosaur Productions and the generosity of dozens of sponsors, Argentina's *Giganotosaurus* "moved in" in June of 2000 . . . followed by *Argentinosaurus* in the spring of 2001. A pair of *Anhanguera* and a group of twenty-one *Pterodaustro* (flying reptiles) also joined the Fernbank "digs" in 2000 and 2001 to round out the Giants of the Mesozoic exhibit. Like most exhibited dinosaur skeletons, these are top-quality fossil casts—exact replicas that make it possible for more museums to display authentic paleontological wonders.

767 Clifton Rd. NE
Atlanta, GA 30307
(404) 929-6300
Web site: http://www.fernbank.edu/museum
E-mail: form on Web site

FERNBANK SCIENCE CENTER

The Fernbank Science Center is actually a huge combination of forests, greenhouses, rose gardens, observatories, planetariums, meteorology labs, and much, much more, but there are dinosaurs on display in the exhibit hall. They simply aren't as lush or exciting as the dinosaurs at the Fernbank Museum. But the whole experience is ideal for young science fans. Check the planetarium schedule for Dinosaur Skies, a special program by exhibit designer Rick C. Spears. Cygnus the Swan and the Big Dipper are easy to find in the night sky. But how about Ptom Pteranodon and the Big Eggshell? Bring your imagination to the planetarium and make new pictures from old star patterns!

156 Heaton Park Dr. NE
Atlanta, GA 30307
(678) 874-7102
Web site: http://www.fernbank.edu
E-mail: fernbank@fernbank.edu

BONE DIGGER BONUS

NESSIE'S COUSIN ALTIE

by Rick C. Spears
Exhibit Designer, Fernbank Science Center

Author's Note: Fernbank Science Center's exhibit designer Rick C. Spears spent years at the Rock Eagle Natural History Museum in Eatonton, Georgia, creating exhibits dinosaur and non-dinosaur alike. He explains his quest for Nessie's cousin the Altamaha-Ha "monster"—and the exhibit he created based on what he found.

In the Rock Eagle Natural History Museum, there was an unused space perfect for a small exhibit. I decided to push the natural history aspect a bit by making the exhibit on cryptozoology . . . something fun and interesting, but based on speculative science. A subject search on the Internet brought the Altamaha-Ha to my attention. I had never heard of this animal, but it has supposedly been sighted for many years around coastal Georgia's Altamaha River. I read all the sighting reports I could find, and based on similarities in those reports, I was able to come up with a portrait of what this mysterious animal might look like:

"Altie" has a gray-green-brown cylindrical body with a long tail that ends in a flattened, diamond shape. Its long neck supports a football-size head, with yellowish eyes and triangular teeth. Its front legs are flippers, but it has no back legs. Its back sports bumps or plates that give it a "tire tread" look. It swims with its powerful tail in an undulating, up and down motion, rather than side to side. This fact, along with sightings during colder months, led me to believe that this animal is a mammal of some sort.

The model I built for the exhibit is of a juvenile Altie, about 10 feet long (adults are reported to be about 20 feet long). I started with a "skeleton" of PVC pipe, surrounded with Styrofoam that is carved into shape. A layer of epoxy-clay "skin," a gray-green-brown paint job, and two glass eyes later, I had a realistic model of the cryptozoological Altie. The model was hung on the wall above a lighted panel that describes the animal and shows its location on a map.

LANIER MUSEUM OF NATURAL HISTORY

Operated by the Gwinnett County Parks and Recreation Division, this small museum exhibits items of natural and cultural historic value. Some trace fossils as well as tracks and a *Triceratops* horn are on display. And don't miss the reptile collection and butterfly garden. Call in advance for tour information.

2601 Buford Dam Rd.

Buford, GA 30518

(404) 932-4460

Web site: NA

E-mail: NA

ROCK EAGLE NATURAL HISTORY MUSEUM

This tiny museum, nestled in the pine forests of rural Eatonton, Georgia, is part of the University of Georgia's 4-H Extension program. It's so little known, the Web site doesn't even feature the remarkable dinosaur exhibits of designer Rick C. Spears. But it should! Spears has created lively, factual reconstruction models of a mother *Albertosaurus* and her hatchlings, a nest of *Protoceratops* babies, a prehistoric marine predator called a mosasaur, and even a plesiosaur-like projection of what Georgia's own "Loch Ness Monster," the Altamaha-Ha, might look like. Spears's work makes Rock Eagle a worthy side trip in the Piedmont area of Georgia.

350 Rock Eagle Rd.

Eatonton, GA 31024

(706) 484-2899

Web site: http://georgia4horg.caes.uga.edu/public/facilities/
    rockeagle/museum.html

E-mail: reagle@uga.edu

Protoceratops

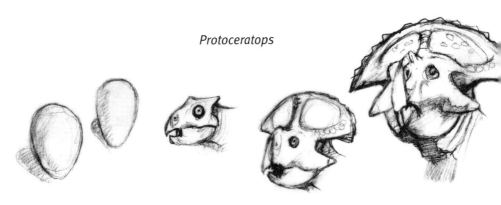

MUSEUM OF ARTS AND SCIENCES

Though you'll find nothing about it on the cool Web site, the Museum of Arts and Sciences in Macon has an 18-foot-long prehistoric whale—a *Zygorhiza*—nicknamed "Ziggy" suspended from the ceiling of the natural history exhibit area. Other marine reptiles native to Georgia are also on display.

> 4182 Forsyth Rd.
>
> Macon, GA 31210
>
> (478) 477-3232
>
> Web site: http://www.masmacon.com
>
> E-mail: info@masmacon.com

WEINMAN MINERAL MUSEUM

To inspire a love of Georgia geology is the primary reason the Weinman Mineral Museum was created. Part of that geology is enough prehistoric evidence to merit a whole "fossil room." Don't miss this fascinating small-town museum's geology collection.

> 51 Mineral Museum Dr.
>
> White, GA 30184
>
> (770) 386-0576
>
> Web site: http://www.weinmanmuseum.org
>
> E-mail: NA

ATLANTA GEOLOGICAL SOCIETY
1455 OLD ALABAMA RD., STE. 170
ROSWELL, GA 30076
WEB SITE: HTTP://WWW.ATLANTAGEOLOGISTS.ORG
E-MAIL: DELYN.THOMPSON@MACTEC.COM (WEBMASTER)

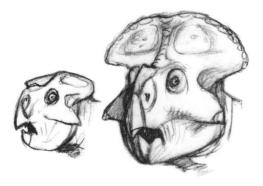

BISHOP MUSEUM

Dr. Neal L. Evenhuis of the museum's Department of Natural Science studies the fossil flies of the world. Part of his findings are posted on the museum's Web site (http://hbs.bishopmuseum.org/fossilcat), and a related booklet catalogs 3,100 different species of ancient flies. From time to time, there may be exhibits at the Bishop Museum to support Dr. Evenhuis's impressive research. There are also marine fossils on display. And watch for traveling dinosaur exhibits, regularly hosted by the Bishop Museum for short periods of time.

> 1525 Bernice St.
> Honolulu, HI 96817
> (808) 847-3511
> Web site: http://www.bishopmuseum.org
> E-mail: webmaster@bishopmuseum.org

HONOLULU COMMUNITY COLLEGE

Thanks to the ambitious energy of this community college paleontology department, there are *finally* dinosaur exhibits in Hawaii! This permanent exhibit of replicas from the American Museum of Natural History in New York includes a *Triceratops* skull, skull and leg bones of *T. rex*, a *Stegosaurus* skeleton, a baby *Hypselosaurus* sculpture, and sculptures of *Iguanodon* and *Deinonychus*. Even if you can't get to Hawaii, be sure you explore the terrific online dinosaur exhibit via the Web site.

> 874 Dillingham Blvd.
> Honolulu, HI 96817
> (808) 845-9211
> Web site: http://www.honolulu.hawaii.edu/dinos/dinos.1.html
> E-mail: form on Web site

Deinonychus

BONE DIGGER BONUS

SHOO, PREHISTORIC FLY

Interview with Dr. Neal L. Evenhuis
Bishop Museum, Department of Natural Science

Author's Note: **Dr. Neal L. Evenhuis helps run the Bishop Museum's Department of Natural Science. And from time to time, the museum benefits from Dr. Evenhuis's remarkable research on prehistoric flies. He has studied more than 3,100 different species of flies that buzzed, swarmed, and pestered during and after the Age of Dinosaurs. What kinds of facts are "flying" around Dr. Evenhuis's head? We asked him a few key questions to try to find out.**

You've studied 3,100 different kinds of ancient flies. Which specimens do you think are the most interesting?

> *Dr. Evenhuis:* **I think the blood-sucking flies (mosquitoes and biting midges) found from Cretaceous deposits (65 million years ago or more) are the most interesting because they needed to feed from warm-blooded animals to survive. The only warm-blooded animals around at that time were very small and rare mammals (the size of small dogs or smaller) and, of course, the more common large dinosaurs.**

From which time periods did the fossil flies come?

> *Dr. Evenhuis:* **Fossil flies are found throughout the known fossil record from the Upper Triassic (about 220 million years ago) to the present. Most of the fossil flies that have been found are from the Eocene and Oligocene (about 30 to 40 million years ago).**

Are ancient flies much like modern-day flies?

> *Dr. Evenhuis:* **They look very similar. There are only very small differences. Yet none of the fossil flies are found around us today. They all have gone extinct.**

Did prehistoric flies pester the dinosaurs the way modern flies pester us?

> *Dr. Evenhuis:* **Those types of flies are actually a very small group of flies, but they are the most visible to us. There are about 120,000 different types of flies in the world today, and many of them are flower pollinators and fungal grazers off of leaf litter in forests, and some (like mosquitoes and tsetse flies) bite and cause diseases. All the various groups of flies occurred in prehistoric times. There is a good chance that the biting flies that were around at the time of the dinosaurs caused diseases in them, as they do in humans and other animals today.**

Were there any prehistoric flies in Hawaii?

> *Dr. Evenhuis:* **None have been found. The lava flows that form our islands are just too young to hold any fossilized insects.**

NATIONAL TROPICAL BOTANICAL GARDEN

Dinosaurs are not a part of Hawaii's geologic history. The state is simply too young in terms of paleo-time. But if you want to capture a glimpse of one of the tropical settings used in the movie *Jurassic Park,* the first film based on Michael Crichton's novel, check out the lovely Allerton Garden in Lawai-kai. It's just one of several lush Hawaiian gardens protected by this organization.

> 3530 Papalina Rd.
> Kalaheo, HI 96741
> (808) 332-7324
> Web site: http://www.ntbg.org
> E-mail: members@ntbg.org

IDAHO

DISCOVERY CENTER OF IDAHO

Though only limited fossil materials are on display full-time, the Discovery Center is committed to bringing traveling exhibits to Boise. Past exhibits have included When Crocodiles Ruled, a show created by the Science Museum of Minnesota that offered a glimpse of the top predator some 60 million years ago—the ferocious prehistoric croc. *That* exhibit is long gone, but look for other stellar dinosaur specials in the months and years to come.

> 131 Myrtle St.
> Boise, ID 83702
> (208) 343-9895
> Web site: http://www.scidaho.org
> E-mail: discoverycenterofidaho@scidaho.org

HAGERMAN FOSSIL BEDS NATIONAL MONUMENT

Not dinosaurs, but prehistoric mammals—lots of them!—were found preserved in this remarkable fossil bed from the Pliocene Epoch. The state fossil, sometimes called the Hagerman Horse, was found in this location. In fact, 120 prehistoric skulls and twenty complete skeletons were discovered in Horse Quarry, one section of this fascinating fossil stop.

PO Box 570
221 N. State St.
Hagerman, ID 83332
(208) 837-4793
Web site: http://www.nps.gov/hafo
E-mail: form on Web site

MUSEUM OF IDAHO

In February 2003, this museum opened, featuring the temporary exhibit of "Sue," the Field Museum of Chicago's *Tyrannosaurus rex* exhibit. By July 2003, the Museum of Idaho unveiled its first major permanent exhibit—a full-size, fleshed-out Colombian mammoth. Committed to bringing outstanding paleontology displays to Idaho Falls, the museum staff promises that's only the beginning. More good things are still to come.

200 N. Eastern Ave.
Idaho Falls, ID 83402
(208) 522-1400
Web site: http://www.museumofidaho.org
E-mail: dnipper@museumofidaho.org

IDAHO MUSEUM OF NATURAL HISTORY

For years, scientists thought dinosaurs didn't live in prehistoric Idaho. Museum Director Linda Deck wants those scientists to know they were wrong, and Dinosaur Times in Idaho—the Idaho Museum of Natural History's exhibit—proves it! Dioramas, skeletal casts, and a mural by gifted paleo-artist Robert Walters examine the dinosaurs that thrived in southeast Idaho 100 million years ago, as well as exploring marine reptiles and other ocean-bound creatures that swam through the prehistoric seas. Also on display are five dinosaur skeletons and other fossil samples, including a neoceratopsian dino (a distant relation of *Triceratops*) exclusive to southeast Idaho.

Campus Box 8096
Fifth Ave. and Dillon St.
ISU Bldg. 12, Rm. 205C
Pocatello, ID 83209
(208) 282-2262
Web site: http://imnh.isu.edu
E-mail: imnh@isu.edu

Neoceratopsian

DINO TIMES IN IDAHO

Interview with Linda Deck
Director, Idaho Museum of Natural History

Author's Note: **For decades, the general public believed there were no dinosaurs to be found in Idaho. Then the experts at the Idaho Museum of Natural History broke the news. Not only did dinosaurs roam the prehistoric territory, they're on display now for all the world to see. We caught up with museum director and paleontologist Linda Deck to get the scoop on Idaho's prehistoric residents.**

When were dinosaurs discovered in southern Idaho? And who discovered them?

Linda Deck: **Paleontologists from the University of Michigan found the first reported dinosaur fossils in Idaho in the mid-1980s.**

What dinosaurs were unearthed at that location?

Linda Deck: **First found were scrappy bones and some teeth. The teeth are tenontosaur (an iguanodontian) and nodosaur (an ankylosaur), and the bones are from a large theropod. Some eggshell material was also discovered. These specimens are from rocks about 100 million years old, from the Early Cretaceous, and therefore provide evidence of a fauna very little studied or known in the United States.**

How were they missed for so long?

Linda Deck: **Idaho doesn't yield its dinosaurs easily. There are no extensive badlands deposits of the right age, such as [those that] exist in Montana, Utah, and Wyoming. Idaho rocks are pretty messed up from mountain-building and erosion, and there are very few exposures of rocks the right age. Furthermore, the sediments that are available tend to be of a type less optimal for bone fossilization.**

Will there be more dinosaur discoveries in Idaho?

Linda Deck: **We're working on it! The exhibit's curator, Ralph Chapman (coincidentally, my husband), who is also a paleontologist, is getting out into the field and expects to understand much more about the potential for more Idaho dinosaurs. The amount we have so far is tantalizingly little of a terrifically diverse fauna. There has got to be more out there, and we intend to go after it.**

What do the people of Idaho think of this new discovery?

Linda Deck: **People of southeastern Idaho are very excited to know that dinosaurs are found locally. Our exhibit has created a lot of interest, and we are seeing many more visitors to our galleries because of it.**

IDAHO GEOLOGICAL SURVEY
MORRILL HALL, THIRD FL.
UNIVERSITY OF IDAHO
PO BOX 443014
MOSCOW, ID 83844
(208) 885-7991
WEB SITE: HTTP://WWW.IDAHOGEOLOGY.ORG
E-MAIL: IGS@UIDAHO.EDU

ILLINOIS

AURORA ART AND HISTORY CENTER

In 1933, when the Civil Works Administration started a federal work project in Aurora, Illinois, they expected to find relief from the financial woes of the Great Depression by creating Phillips Park Lake. Unearthing prehistoric mastodon remains was something the 555-man crew never expected! The 10,000-to-22,000-year-old prehistoric elephant relative they found is exhibited at the Aurora Art and History Center.

> 20 E. Downer Pl.
> Aurora, IL 60505
> (630) 906-0650
> Web site: http://www.aurorahistoricalsociety.org/museums.html
> E-mail: form on Web site

MASTODON RECREATION AREA

When you're in Aurora, Illinois, don't miss your chance to visit the Mastodon Peninsula site on Mastodon Island in Phillips Park. It showcases a life-size mastodon sculpture along with an interactive exhibit for young people. Mastodon footprints, a tusk maze, and a mastodon slide make this a playground as well as an educational adventure.

> (Phillips Park on Wyeth Dr.)
> Aurora, IL 60507
> (630) 898-7228
> Web site: http://www.aurora-il.org
> E-mail: NA

THE FIELD MUSEUM

Paleontologist Peter Larson and his crew at the Black Hills Institute first excavated the magnificent (and nearly complete) *Tyrannosaurus rex* specimen we call "Sue" from the rugged badlands of South Dakota. Today, Sue is on display, carefully restored, at the Field Museum in Chicago, thanks in part to McDonald's and Walt Disney World, who helped buy her at auction. Sue is the crown jewel of the Field Museum's paleontological collection, but not their only treasure. It's a first-rate museum not to be missed.

BONE DIGGER BONUS

NEW OLD FOSSILS

by William F. Simpson
Collections Manager, Fossil Vertebrates
The Field Museum

All of our skeletons were fairly recently moved from the old hall to the new hall. Many, including dinosaurs such as Apatosaurus, *were remounted in more lifelike poses. It was my job to make sure the fossil bones were handled properly and not broken during the process.*

When the new exhibit opened in the summer of 1994, my bones looked even more exciting than when I first saw them, many years ago.

Mounting the gigantic Brachiosaurus *skeleton was also exciting. We have had the skeleton for which the whole species was named since 1900, when the Field Museum dug up the bones in Colorado. But this is a very incomplete skeleton and a little hard to understand without more bones.*

We finally decided to erect a complete fiberglass copy of a Brachiosaurus *so that people would understand what they were looking at when they saw the real bones on display next to it.*

Again, it was my job to look out for the safety of the real fossils. I supervised the restoration and the molding of the duplicate bones. The missing portion of the skeleton was based on a more complete Brachiosaurus *found by German scientists in Africa.*

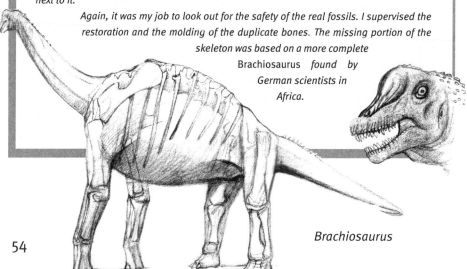

Brachiosaurus

1400 S. Lake Shore Dr.

Chicago, IL 60605

(312) 922-9410

Web site: http://www.fmnh.org

E-mail: webmaster@fieldmuseum.org

PEGGY NOTEBAERT NATURE MUSEUM

Though there are roughly 30,000 fossils in the Chicago Academy of Sciences' collection, the most important subgroup consists of 8,000 Silurian fossils from the Chicago region collected by William C. Egan between 1870 and 1890. There are about seventy type specimens—fossils of such exceptional quality they define the standard against which other fossils are measured. Also in the collection are Mazon Creek insects, Carboniferous plants, and about two dozen casts of vertebrate fossils.

Chicago Academy of Sciences

2430 N. Cannon Dr.

Chicago, IL 60614

(773) 755-5100

Web site: http://www.chias.org

E-mail: form on Web site

WESTERN ILLINOIS UNIVERSITY MUSEUM OF GEOLOGY

When it was founded in 1975, the WIU Museum of Geology was meant to be a teaching museum—a tool for geology students to use to better their understanding of the natural world. But the exhibits were so engaging, the general public began to embrace the collection. Today, more than forty exhibits and displays covering the ancient Illinois coal swamps, the Ice Age, dinosaurs, and other non-prehistoric mineral treasures are open for all students of geology to explore. It's a terrific little gem in the heart of Macomb.

Tillman Hall

1 University Circle

Macomb, IL 61455

(309) 298-1368

Web site: http://www.wiu.edu/users/migeol/museum.htm

E-mail: RE-Johnson2@wiu.edu (Robert Johnson, curator)

LAKEVIEW MUSEUM

Expect outstanding dinosaur exhibits on loan, including the remarkable Dinosaurs Versus Meteorites exhibit, and other fossil studies.

1125 W. Lake Ave.

Peoria, IL 61614

(309) 686-7000

Web site: http://www.lakeview-museum.org

E-mail: aschmitt@lakeview-museum.org (Ann Schmitt,
   associate director of education)

BURPEE MUSEUM OF NATURAL HISTORY

Out of the Rock: A Prehistoric Journey is the Burpee Museum's dinosaur exhibit. A look back at all of ancient history, the journey begins more than 4 billion years ago with the big bang theory, then takes you through the origins of life, an ancient sea, prehistoric coal forests, and, eventually, past a 39-foot *Tyrannosaurus rex* mounted in a crouching, predatory pose.

737 N. Main St.

Rockford, IL 61103

(815) 965-3433

Web site: http://www.burpee.org

E-mail: info@burpee.org

ILLINOIS STATE MUSEUM

Exhibits about the science of Ice Age changes and the fossils of Mazon Creek are just part of the prehistoric treasures on display at the Illinois State Museum. Why are the fossils of Mazon Creek worth exploring? Most bone beds yield only bones—mineralized prehistoric skeletal pieces. But Mazon Creek's soft sediment helped preserve more than ancient bone. It helped preserve soft tissue as well, giving us a better picture of prehistoric Springfield.

Spring and Edwards streets

Springfield, IL 62706

(217) 782-7387

Web site: http://www.museum.state.il.us

E-mail: webmaster@museum.state.il.us

ILLINOIS STATE GEOLOGICAL SURVEY

615 E. PEABODY DR.

CHAMPAIGN, IL 61820

(217) 333-4747

WEB SITE: HTTP://WWW.ISGS.UIUC.EDU/ISGSHOME.HTML

E-MAIL: ISGS@ISGS.UIUC.EDU

FALLS OF THE OHIO STATE PARK

Fifty years ago, farsighted scientists and concerned citizens started an effort to protect the rich fossil resources of Falls of the Ohio State Park. Mineralized records of life 360 to 430 million years ago were scattered across 550 acres. The $5 million visitors center—which features more than forty-eight exhibits—is only part of the conservation effort. After a fifteen-minute video introduction in the center's 102-seat auditorium, you're set free to experience dozens of amazing displays. You'll see a full-size mammoth, murals, and the 4-foot-tall skull of *Dunkleosteus,* a Devonian fish that was 30 feet long, nose to tail. Outside the interpretive center, you'll see the massive bone beds themselves, still actively harvested today by paleontologists. During the summer months, children nine to fourteen can actually participate in Young Paleontologist Camps—hiking, mapping fossil beds, and collecting, cleaning, and cataloging fossils—for a very reasonable fee.

> 201 W. Riverside Dr.
> Clarksville, IN 47129
> (812) 280-9970
> Web site: http://www.fallsoftheohio.org
> E-mail: park@fallsoftheohio.org

THE CHILDREN'S MUSEUM OF INDIANAPOLIS

Indiana may have been underwater during the day of the dinosaur, but you'd never know it looking at this museum's incredible hands-on exhibit, Dinosphere. It is truly one of the most remarkable paleontology offerings for young people in the world, thanks to the genius and feedback of bone-hunting advisors, including Robert T. Bakker, Phil Currie, Pete Larson, and Paul Sereno. Look for lab and dig simulations, as well as dinosaur skeletons and models—almost *anything* related to the science of paleontology is covered in Dinosphere. Also at the museum is the Natural World exhibit of prehistoric marine fossils and a mastodon found in 1976.

> 3000 N. Meridian St.
> Indianapolis, IN 46208
> (317) 334-3322
> Web site: http://www.childrensmuseum.org
> E-mail: communic@childrensmuseum.org

Tyrannosaurus rex

BONE DIGGER BONUS

ALL IN THE DINOSAUR FAMILY

(Courtesy of the Children's Museum of Indianapolis)

The opening of the new Paleo Prep Lab launched the creation of the $25 million Dinosphere—a one-of-a-kind dinosaur experience for children and families at the Children's Museum of Indianapolis.

In the Paleo Prep Lab, children can begin their search for dinosaur clues through in-depth educational programs that will allow them to work side by side with professional preparators to clean and prepare 65-million-year-old dinosaur fossils for display in Dinosphere.

"Nothing captures a child's imagination and curiosity more than dinosaurs. Our Paleo Prep Lab begins the process of engaging children in the Earth's Cretaceous Period—the last period before dinosaurs became extinct," says Dr. Jeffrey H. Patchen, president and CEO of the Children's Museum of Indianapolis.

Living true to the Children's Museum's mission to "create extraordinary learning experiences that have the power to transform the lives of children and families," Dinosphere features one of the largest displays of real juvenile and family dinosaur fossils in the United States. According to paleontologist Dr. Robert Bakker, it quickly earned its place "among the top dozen dinosaur exhibits in the world" and is "the most exciting new addition on the list of real-bone dinosaur exhibits." Through this immersive exhibit, children and families will truly experience how dinosaurs lived more than 65 million years ago.

Dr. Patchen added, "By introducing children to the world of dinosaurs, the museum also compels children to explore the world of science. The entire notion of extinction 65 million years ago and what extinction for endangered animals and plants means today will play a major part of the exhibit.

"The centerpiece of Dinosphere is 'Bucky,' a teenage Tyrannosaurus rex—the fourth-most-complete T. rex ever found—whose acquisition was made possible through the Scott A. Jones Foundation. We also have a nearly complete Gorgosaurus skeleton; 'Baby Louie,' the only fully articulated dinosaur embryo fossil ever found in the world (which was featured on the cover of National Geographic); and 'Kelsey,' one of the most complete Triceratops skeletons known to science, just to name a few."

Tyrannosaurus rex and Torosaurus

INDIANA STATE MUSEUM

Indiana was underwater during the time the dinosaurs ruled, but the fossil record is still rich and complete at this Indianapolis museum. Don't miss the Ice Age exhibits—including one of the most extensive prehistoric tooth collections in the world—along with mammoth and mastodon remains donated by local farmers, who often found them while planting their crops. Online, the museum's "Indiana Story" slide show offers a terrific overview of the prehistoric past of the Hoosier state, including an ancient sea, an Ice Age, and man's debut on Indiana soil.

> 650 W. Washington St.
> Indianapolis, IN 46204
> (317) 232-1637
> Web site: http://www.in.gov/ism
> E-mail: museumcommunication@dnr.in.gov

JOSEPH MOORE MUSEUM

Prehistoric skeletons—including carnivorous *Allosaurus*; a giant, extinct beaver called *Castoroides ohioensis;* a giant ground sloth called *Megalonyx jeffersonii;* a mastodon; and the skull of *Smilodon,* a saber-toothed cat—are all a part of this academic natural history museum's fossil resources. But you'll also find hundreds of prehistoric marine fossils from beneath an ancient sea.

> Earlham College
> 801 National Rd. W.
> Richmond, IN 47374
> (765) 983-1303
> Web site: http://www.earlham.edu/~biol/jmmuseum
> E-mail: johni@earlham.edu (John Iverson, museum director)

INDIANA GEOLOGICAL SURVEY
611 N. WALNUT GROVE
BLOOMINGTON, IN 47405
(812) 855-7636
WEB SITE: HTTP://IGS.INDIANA.EDU
E-MAIL: IGSINFO@INDIANA.EDU

THE PUTNAM MUSEUM OF HISTORY AND NATURAL SCIENCE

This small but well-organized museum features many aspects of history and science, including a hands-on fossil exhibit in its River Valley Discovery Room.

> 1717 W. Twelfth St.
> Davenport, IA 52804
> (563) 324-1933
> Web site: http://www.putnam.org
> E-mail: museum@putnam.org

IOWA HISTORICAL MUSEUM

Fossils are only a minor part of the Iowa Historical Museum's exhibits. But what is on display represents the vast ocean that covered the state during prehistoric times. The Delicate Balance: Human Values and Iowa's Natural Resources exhibit features a cross section of those marine fossils, including crinoids, for which Iowa is famous. Same Time, Different Place is a marine aquarium display that offers a miniature glimpse at that warm, shallow prehistoric sea. You might also enjoy Crystal Treasures, a collection of crystals found in Iowa coal mines, and Geode, a stunning look at the official Iowa state rock.

> 600 E. Locust
> Des Moines, IA 50319
> (515) 281-5111
> Web site: http://www.iowahistory.org/museum
> E-mail: NA

CORALVILLE LAKE SPILLWAY/DEVONIAN FOSSIL GORGE

In July 1993, the Coralville Dam failed and the lake overflowed, creating an emergency spillway that flowed for twenty-eight days. The 15-foot gorge created by the flow of floodwaters revealed an amazing snapshot of Devonian Iowa— an underwater environment 375 million years old, reflected in a wealth of fossilized remains. Don't expect dinosaurs but rather tiny sea creatures, including brachiopods, crinoids, bryozoans, corals, and trilobites. The nearby lake campgrounds include picnic tables, a playground, and groomed hiking trails.

Megatherium

2850 Prairie du Chien Rd. NE
Iowa City, IA 52240
(319) 338-3543
Web site: http://www.mvr.usace.army.mil/Coralville/default.htm
Alternate Web site: http://www.north-liberty.com/recreation/
    fossils.htm
E-mail: Kathryn.S.Atkinson@usace.army.mil

THE UNIVERSITY OF IOWA MUSEUM OF NATURAL HISTORY

Take a 500-million-year journey through Iowa's past in the Iowa Hall of this university museum. Explore a prehistoric Devonian coral reef through a dramatic diorama, featuring *Dunkleosteus,* a ferocious carnivore that could grow to be nearly 30 feet long. Move on to a 300-million-year-old Pennsylvanian Period coal swamp, again represented as a diorama. As the waters receded, prehistoric mammals like the giant, 10-foot-long Ice Age sloth (discovered by Thomas Jefferson) grazed Iowa's new lands. A diorama and model capture the wonders of this mammal that went extinct 9,500 years ago.

10 Macbride Hall
Iowa City, IA 52242
(319) 335-0480
Web site: http://www.uiowa.edu/~nathist
E-mail: NA

BONE DIGGER BONUS

A FLOOD OF GOOD FORTUNE

We usually think of floods—walls of powerful, unexpected water—as strokes of bad luck. But when a flood drenched the spillway at Coralville Lake near Iowa City, Iowa, in 1993, it washed away the barriers of time and revealed a treasure trove of Devonian fossil secrets 375 million years in the making.

According to Jean Cutler Prior's Coralville Lake visitors guide, "It is now possible to walk across acres of Devonian-age seafloors and get a firsthand look at features normally hidden from view or glimpsed only in vertical cuts along roadsides or in quarries. The exposed rocks provide a rare opportunity for public observation of Iowa's geologic past."

Among the discoveries you'll see are the fossilized remains of ancient sea life that swam the shallow Devonian sea that covered much of Iowa; coral beds—some turned topsy-turvy by an ancient storm; sea lilies (called crinoids); and evidence of burrowing worms and trilobites.

FOSSIL AND PRAIRIE CENTER FOUNDATION

The sleepy town of Rockford has long been known as the home of Devonian fossils. Since the 1800s, thousands of fossil fans have visited the 400-acre park now owned and carefully managed by the Floyd County Conservation Board. Working together with the Fossil and Prairie Center Foundation, it has developed a plan, via an educational study center, to preserve and highlight the rich prehistoric legacy for generations to come.

> 1227 215th St.
>
> Rockford, IA 50468
>
> (641) 756-3490
>
> Web site: http://www.fossilcenter.com
>
> E-mail: fpcenter@omnitelcom.com

MADISON COUNTY MUSEUM COMPLEX

When Amel Priest decided to donate his substantial collection of Iowa invertebrate fossils, three museums offered to lovingly care for the specimens. But Priest spent decades in Madison County collecting the treasures. So Madison County, he thought, was where they should stay. Don't miss exploring his crinoids and other marine-animal fossils when you're in Winterset.

> 815 S. Second Ave.
>
> PO Box 15
>
> Winterset, IA 50273
>
> (515) 462-2134
>
> Web site: NA
>
> E-mail: mchistoricalsociety1@juno.com

IOWA GEOLOGICAL SURVEY
109 TROWBRIDGE HALL
IOWA CITY, IA 52242
(319) 335-1575
WEB SITE: HTTP://WWW.IGSB.UIOWA.EDU
E-MAIL: WEBMANAGER@IGSB.UIOWA.EDU

JOHNSTON GEOLOGY MUSEUM

Dr. Paul Johnston worked for thirty-eight years in the ESU Earth Science Department. That dedication won him a grand tribute, as well as the respect of his students and peers. The museum named for Johnston includes forty-five displays from the world-famous Hamilton Quarry, as well as mosasaurs, a giant ground sloth, mastodon tusks, and petrified wood.

> Emporia State University
> Cram Science Hall
> Fourteenth Ave. and Merchant St.
> Emporia, KS 66801
> (620) 341-5330
> Web site: http://www.emporia.edu/earthsci/museum/
>   museum.htm
> E-mail: moralesm@emporia.edu

STERNBERG MUSEUM OF NATURAL HISTORY

Picture 3 *million* fossil specimens—from tiny marine plants, ammonites, fish, and mosasaurs that thrived in a shallow prehistoric sea over Kansas to the most important collection of pterosaurs, or flying reptiles, in the world—and you have an idea of how amazing the Sternberg Museum's paleontological collection actually is. Now remember why the name Sternberg is so familiar in terms of the history of fossil collecting and you'll have an even better idea of why the museum is so special. The Sternberg family—father Charles and sons George, Charlie, and Levi—changed the face of American paleontology with their amazing instinct for finding dinosaurs. Even the first three mummified dinosaur fossils were unearthed by the Sternbergs! This Kansas museum is more than a great fossil find—it's a page of paleontological history.

> 3000 Sternberg Dr.
> Hays, KS 67601
> (877) 332-1165
> Web site: http://www.fhsu.edu/sternberg
> E-mail: mkellerm@fhsu.edu

KINGMAN COUNTY MUSEUM

This historic building—a turn-of-the-century government office and firehouse built in 1888—is worth visiting just for its architectural beauty. But this isn't a book about pretty buildings. It's a book about fossil exhibits. So slip into the

BONE DIGGER BONUS

CRETACEOUS KANSAS:
HOME OF THE REAL SEA MONSTER

by Mike Everhardt
Oceans of Kansas Paleontology
http://www.oceansofkansas.com

During the Late Cretaceous Period in the Age of Dinosaurs, there were real sea monsters in the shallow ocean that covered Kansas and most of the middle of North America. About 100 million years ago, a giant plesiosaur called Brachauchenius lucasi *would have been one of the largest and most dangerous creatures living in the ocean.* Brachauchenius *is a "short-neck" plesiosaur (or pliosaur) because it only had twelve or thirteen vertebrae in its neck. A long-neck plesiosaur like* Elasmosaurus *had as many as seventy-two vertebrae in its neck, but its head was very small. Its jaws were about 6 feet long. There were more than twenty teeth in each jaw, some of which were more than 4 inches long.*

In fact, the skull and jaws of Brachauchenius *were almost as large as those of* Tyrannosaurus rex. *A fully grown* Brachauchenius *would have been between 30 and 35 feet long, or about the length of an average school bus. These pliosaurs grew to be almost as large as the largest predatory dinosaurs that lived on the land.*

Both pliosaurs and plesiosaurs used their large, paddle-like limbs to "fly" through the water like huge, underwater birds as they searched for food. The giant pliosaurs spent their whole lives swimming in the ocean, where they fed upon squid, fish, other marine reptiles like turtles and ichthyosaurs, and even plesiosaurs.

When a big pliosaur like Brachauchenius *was hunting for a meal, he would probably swim toward his prey and then dive deep enough so that he was approaching from underneath. The pliosaur could easily see his victim against the sunlit surface of the ocean, but he could not be seen in the dark water below. Then he would swim quickly upward, and at the last moment, open his large, tooth-filled jaws and seize his prey. Once his jaws closed, it was all over. Usually the force of his powerful bite was enough to kill his prey instantly. When he was sure the prey was dead, the pliosaur would move it around in his mouth so that it was pointed headfirst into his throat. This was especially important when the pliosaur was eating fish because the sharp spines in the fish's fins would stick in his throat if it was swallowed backward. Once it was in position, it was quickly swallowed. Unless it was a large animal, the pliosaur would probably swim off to find another victim.*

There are three known specimens of Brachauchenius. *The first one was found in Kansas over a hundred years ago. Another was discovered in Texas in 1907. The third and largest one was collected in 1950 from Russell County in central Kansas. The skull is on exhibit in the Sternberg Museum of Natural History in Hays, Kansas.*

Kingman County Museum to check out the prehistoric hip bone and other bits and pieces left behind by a giant mastodon, as well as the other mysterious ancient animal fossils also found in local Kansas fields. Don't expect huge numbers of fossils, but you'll find a few bones if you take the time to look.

400 N. Main St.

Kingman, KS 67068

(620) 532-5274

Web site: http://www.skyways.kumc.edu/genweb/kingman/
    museum.html

E-mail: kingmanhistory@aol.com

POST ROCK MUSEUM

Housed in a native stone cabin built by homesteader Dan Haley in 1883, this museum is actually a tribute to the pioneer spirit and the limestone blocks and construction that helped it endure when the state was wild and untamed. Houses weren't the only structures made of limestone. Fence posts, tombstones, walkways, windowsills, and many other ordinary items were made of the stone. It was soft and easily drilled when it first came out of the ground, but hard and durable once the open air helped it set. But long before eighteenth-century pioneers dug up limestone to make their lives a little easier, prehistoric fossils were preserved in the slabs. The Post Rock Museum will soon open an exhibit dedicated to the region's limestone. If you're in LaCrosse, call the museum to see if the exhibit has been completed.

202 W. First St.

LaCrosse, KS 67548

(785) 222-2719

Web site: http://www.rushcounty.org/postrockmuseum

E-mail: NA

THE UNIVERSITY OF KANSAS NATURAL HISTORY MUSEUM

Though this fine teaching museum has several excellent fossil collections, the most exciting dinosaur news and exhibits revolve around the KU Vertebrate Paleontology's dig adventure in Wyoming. In the summers of 1997 and 1998, the dig team discovered a sauropod bone bed with several long-necked, 145-million-year-old plant-eating dinosaurs nestled within it. Two adults—"Lyle" and "Annabelle"—and a juvenile—"Nic-Mic"—were excavated side by side, something never before unearthed by paleontologists. The adult skeletons are nearly complete, but the young specimen is not. Local volunteers are invited to help prepare, or clean, these fossils, removing the stone matrix from the actual fossilized bone to be displayed at the university museum.

1345 Jayhawk Blvd.
Lawrence, KS 66045
(785) 864-4450
Web site: http://www.nhm.ku.edu
E-mail: kunhm@ku.edu

McPHERSON MUSEUM

Though more local history than fossils, you will find the fossil remains of Ice Age mammals common to Kansas in the McPherson Museum, including ground sloths, saber-toothed cats, and marine animals.

1130 E. Euclid St.
McPherson, KS 67460
(620) 241-8464
Web site: NA
E-mail: NA

FICK FOSSIL AND HISTORY MUSEUM

Earnest and Vi Fick loved fossils, and they loved Oakley, Kansas. So it's only natural that they donated their extensive collection of Cretaceous treasures to the Fick Fossil and History Museum. Most of the specimens were collected within 50 miles of the town. Since Kansas was underwater during the Cretaceous, that means you'll find marine reptile remains from the giant fish *Xiphactinus*, plesiosaurs, and mosasaurs, as well as smaller marine animals like crinoids and coral. You'll also find more recent prehistoric mammals that flourished as the sea receded, including Oligocene rhinoceros. Bored with fossils? (Yeah, right!) Check out the Kansas Wildflower Collection, also housed at the Fick Fossil and History Museum.

700 W. Third St.
Oakley, KS 67748
(785) 672-4839
Web site: http://www.discoveroakley.com
E-mail: fickmuseum@ruraltel.net

KANSAS GEOLOGICAL SURVEY
1930 CONSTANT AVE.
LAWRENCE, KS 66047
(785) 864-3965
WEB SITE: HTTP://WWW.KGS.KU.EDU
E-MAIL: WEBADMIN@KGS.KU.EDU

KENTUCKY COAL MINING MUSEUM

This museum is focused on mining, not fossils. So don't expect much when it comes to prehistoric resources. But they do have a small collection that includes *Alethopteris* (seed ferns), the fossil horsetail *Calamites* and related *Sphenophyllum*, and fossil trilobites. So why not check it out if you're in Benham?

> 221 Main St.
> Benham, KY 40807
> (606) 848-1530
> Web site: http://www.kingdomcome.org/museum
> E-mail: form on Web site

EXPLORIUM OF LEXINGTON

Formerly known as the Lexington Children's Museum, the Explorium of Lexington is one of the United States' oldest children's museums. For years, the museum has had a great display of fossils, including a prehistoric cave-bear skeleton. But it recently got a real treasure from Walter Gross, a private collector and vice president of Pepsi-Cola of Lexington—a replica of the skull of "Stan," a *Tyrannosaurus rex* unearthed by Pete Larson and the Black Hills Institute of Geological Research in Hill City, South Dakota.

> Victorian Square
> 440 W. Short St.
> Lexington, KY 40507
> (859) 258-3253
> Web site: http://www.explorium.com
> E-mail: explore@explorium.com

CLEMENT MINERAL MUSEUM

Included among the mineral collection of the late Ben E. Clement are some Kentucky fossil specimens, but the Clement Mineral Museum is mostly full of spectacular examples of crystals and rocks of many kinds. The Web site offers dozens of stunning photographs as a taste of what's on display. But nothing will compare to seeing the minerals for yourself.

> 205 N. Walker St.
> Marion, KY 42064
> (877) 965-4263
> (270) 965-4263

Web site: http://www.clementmineralmuseum.org

E-mail: beclement@kynet.biz

BLUE LICKS BATTLEFIELD STATE PARK

Perhaps best known as the site of the last battle of the Revolutionary War in Kentucky (in 1782—Daniel Boone's son was a casualty), this state park is also the site of a prehistoric mastodon bone bed. The on-site museum celebrates both of the park's claims to fame through exhibits and video presentations.

Hwy. 68 (48 miles northeast of Lexington)

Mt. Olivet, KY 41064

(800) 443-7008

Web site: http://www.state.ky.us/agencies/parks/bluelick.htm

E-mail: bluelicks@ky.gov

OWENSBORO MUSEUM OF SCIENCE AND HISTORY

A magnificent prehistoric elephant graces the OMSH logo and Web site for good reason. It's part of the paleontology collection on exhibit at the 90,000-square-foot museum founded in 1966 and moved to an expansive downtown location in 1994. Also on display is a collection of live reptiles.

122 E. Second St.

Owensboro, KY 42303

(270) 687-2732

Web site: http://www.owensboromuseum.com

E-mail: information@owensboromuseum.com

BIG BONE LICK STATE PARK

Imagine the age of the prehistoric mammal—a time 12,000 to 20,000 years ago, when huge mammoths and ground sloths roamed the open landscape. Imagine they join mastodons and bison striding through swamps and mineral springs. An unlucky few get bogged down, trapped in the oxygen-starved marshes. They starve or drown, sink, and are covered . . . fossilized in sulfur and secret, until the 1700s when they are found. You're imagining what could be a scene from prehistoric Big Bone Lick State Park—a dig site often credited as the "birthplace of American vertebrate paleontology." No dinosaurs, but exciting science nonetheless.

3380 Beaver Rd.

Union, KY 41091

(859) 384-3522

Web site: http://www.state.ky.us/agencies/parks/bigbone.htm

E-mail: BigBoneLick@ky.gov

BONE DIGGER BONUS

BIG BONE LICKED

by Robert D. Lindy
Big Bone Lick State Park

In prehistoric times, great herds of giant mastodons, mammoths, bison, primitive horses, and sloths lived in north-central Kentucky. The huge beasts, attracted to the salt found in abundance in the swampland, got stuck in the ooze and died.

When American Indians guided French explorer Charles Le Moyne de Longueuil to Big Bone Lick in 1739, bones were still lying on the marshy ground.

By 1840, it was estimated that the bones of hundreds of mammals had been removed from the area, which today has many bones and research materials on display in the museum. The warm salt springs are still visible as well.

Visitors are introduced to the fascinating history of Big Bone Lick in a museum with displays of ancient bones and a video presentation about the history of Big Bone Lick. An outdoor museum contains life-size models of the prehistoric mastodon and bison, the last remaining salt sulfur spring, and a model dig site that contains bone samples and replicas. A live herd of modern buffalo is also on display.

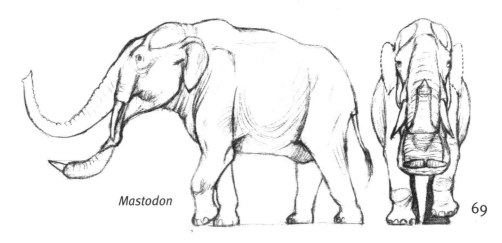

Mastodon

69

LOUISIANA

THE LOUISIANA MUSEUM OF NATURAL HISTORY

The front third of a prehistoric whale, *Basilosaurus*, is just one of the treasures within the vertebrate paleontology collection at the Louisiana Museum of Natural History. Also on display are fossilized elephants, camels, bats, hedgehogs, and horses. Cretaceous dinosaur specimens are also part of the museum's collection.

119 Foster Hall

Louisiana State University

Baton Rouge, LA 70803

(225) 578-2855

Web site: http://www.lsu.edu/museum

E-mail: museum@lsu.edu

LSU MUSEUM OF NATURAL SCIENCE

When the museum (a component of the Louisiana Museum of Natural History) was founded in 1936, it was focused on bird specimens for classroom application. Since then, it's collected 2.5 million specimens that include exhibits on zoology, archaeology, and paleontology.

119 Foster Hall

Louisiana State University

Baton Rouge, LA 70803

(225) 578-2855

Web site: http://www.lsu.edu/museum

E-mail: museum@lsu.edu

TULANE UNIVERSITY MUSEUM OF NATURAL HISTORY

Tulane officials describe their paleontology collection as "modest" and say it reflects mainly marine vertebrates donated by the New Orleans Academy of Science in 1885. It is available for study by appointment only. But it is there.

Bldg. A-3, Wild Boar Rd.

Belle Chasse, LA 70037

(504) 394-1711

Web site: http://www.museum.tulane.edu

E-mail: hank@museum.tulane.edu

LAFAYETTE NATURAL HISTORY MUSEUM AND PLANETARIUM

Lots of great science exhibits are on display at this Louisiana museum. But the best place for fossils is the kid-friendly Discovery Room, where a small collection of fossils is presented in a hands-on exhibit, along with a mounted skeleton of a sei whale.

433 Jefferson St.
Lafayette, LA 70501
(337) 291-5544
Web site: http://www.lnhm.org
E-mail: NA

MUSEUM OF NATURAL HISTORY

Thanks to the generosity of benefactors, this educational museum received more than 5,000 specimens from the B. C. Marshall reptile and amphibian collection, bringing the total number of specimens up to 55,000. More than 75,000 cataloged fish specimens, both contemporary and prehistoric, are also part of the museum's collection. Only a fraction of the material on exhibit is fossilized. But it's an amazing way to explore the past and how it relates to the present.

308 Sandal Hall
College of Arts and Sciences
University of Louisiana at Monroe
Monroe, LA 71209
(318) 342-3299
Web site: http://www.ulm.edu/~pezold/welcome.htm
E-mail: NA

BONE DIGGER BONUS

FOSSIL MAMMALVILLE

by Dr. Judith A. Schiebout
Associate Curator, LSU Museum of Natural Science

Louisiana doesn't have extensive open badlands for fossil hunting or exposures of terrestrial rocks the right age to yield dinosaurs. But we do recover some fossil mammals, in part by counting on the help of ordinary people who encounter something unusual.

I recall with gratitude the Corps of Engineers, who supported excavation at an Eocene marine site in the center of the state and helped out by lifting the field cast of a beautiful skull of a primitive whale, Basilosaurus, up a steep bluff on a bulldozer blade. Careful preparation of this specimen in our lab yielded even the tiny inner-ear bones.

Another lucky find came about when a local developer was digging a cooling pond and the bulldozer operator hit bone—a mastodon. He reported the find, and work was halted to allow us to excavate.

AUDUBON NATURE INSTITUTE

For years, the Audubon Nature Institute's Pathways to the Past exhibit detailed theories of evolution (including how birds evolved from dinosaurs) through hands-on exhibits, engaging dinosaur models, and other educational displays housed in a special building. The institute was closed in 2005 following Hurricane Katrina, but plans to rebuild. Call in advance for information.

5700 Read Blvd.
New Orleans, LA 70127
(800) 774-7394
(504) 246-5672
Web site: http://www.auduboninstitute.org
E-mail: air@auduboninstitute.org

LOUISIANA GEOLOGICAL SURVEY
3079 ENERGY, COAST AND ENVIRONMENTAL BLDG.
LOUISIANA STATE UNIVERSITY
BATON ROUGE, LA 70803
(225) 578-5320
WEB SITE: HTTP://WWW.LGS.LSU.EDU
E-MAIL: HAMMER@LSU.EDU

Mammoth

MAINE STATE MUSEUM

Exploring Maine's prehistory—at least that of the past 12,000 years—is easy thanks to an exhibit at the Maine State Museum, aptly entitled 12,000 Years in Maine. Fossilized remains of a prehistoric walrus and a woolly mammoth offer a glimpse into Ice Age Maine. And a remarkable cache of Paleo-Indian material brings those ancient people to life.

> 83 State House Station
> Augusta, ME 04333
> (207) 287-2301
> Web site: http://www.state.me.us/museum
> E-mail: maine.museum@maine.gov

BONE DIGGER BONUS

A MAMMOTH IN MAINE

by Gary Hoyle
Retired Curator of the Maine State Museum

Studying the first discovery of a woolly mammoth in Maine has been a fascinating project, not only because it proves this ancient elephant lived in more locations than we thought, but because like all good scientific investigations, it generates important questions.

Because of years of water erosion and the scouring action of ancient continental glaciers, all traces of dinosaurs and early vertebrates have been stripped from the landmass that became Maine. Nevertheless, about 13,000 years ago, while the last glacier was retreating, the remains of a few vertebrates became trapped in the sediment released by melting ice.

There is a long-held theory that the enormous weight of the mile-thick glacier pushed the land below sea level, then melted away faster than the land could bounce back. Consequently, ocean water followed the retreating glacier many miles inland and covered much of the state of Maine for up to 1,000 years.

However, the discovery of the mammoth bones in clay containing seashells tells us the story of Maine's postglacial environment was not so simple. The woolly mammoth was a grazer in grasslands. Where were the grasslands in Maine at the time? How did this creature—which we nicknamed "Hairy-It"—die? Did humans butcher it? Were humans even in Maine at the time?

We hope that further research at the Maine State Museum will answer these and other prehistoric questions.

THE NORTHERN MAINE MUSEUM OF SCIENCE

Partially recovered when Portland, Maine's museum closed, these exhibits represent a work in progress at the University of Maine's Presque Isle campus. Expect to see a pterosaur model with a 9-foot wingspan, along with an exhibit that explores the dinosaur-bird theory of evolution. Also on display are trilobites, fossil fish, mammoths, and an *Ichthyosaurus* cast.

University of Maine at Presque Isle

181 Main St.

Presque Isle, ME 04769

(207) 768-9482

Web site: http://www.umpi.maine.edu/info/nmms/museum.htm

E-mail: mccartney@polaris.umpi.maine.edu (Kevin McCartney, museum director)

MAINE GEOLOGICAL SURVEY
22 STATE HOUSE STATION
AUGUSTA, ME 04333
(207) 287-2801
WEB SITE: HTTP://WWW.STATE.ME.US/DOC/NRIMC/MGS/MGS.HTM
E-MAIL: MGS@MAINE.GOV

MARYLAND

MARYLAND SCIENCE CENTER

Dinosaur Mysteries, the Maryland Science Center's outstanding paleontology exhibit, features a hands-on approach to exploring prehistoric life and theory. There are two dozen dinosaur skeletons to examine, interactive exhibits about dinosaur hearing, a 7-foot dinosaur nest you can curl up in, and more. A wonderful array of dinosaur options for the entire family.

601 Light St.

Baltimore, MD 21230

(410) 685-5225

Web site: http://www.mdsci.org

E-mail: guestservices@marylandsciencecenter.org

CALVERT CLIFFS STATE PARK

For a time, visitors could hike a trail along the Calvert Cliffs, collecting samples of prehistoric fossils straight from rocky walls 15 million years in the making. Today, the same erosion that revealed more than 600 different fossilized species makes it too dangerous to hike the old trail. But visitors are still welcome to stroll the open beach in search of the tiny ocean fossils—including shark teeth—which they can keep. Located 14 miles south of Prince Fredrick, be prepared for a 2-mile hike from the parking lot.

c/o Smallwood State Park

2750 Sweden Point Rd.

Marbury, MD 20658

(301) 743-7613

Web site: http://www.dnr.state.md.us/publiclands/southern/
calvertcliffs.html

E-mail: NA

BONE DIGGER BONUS

CALVERT CLIFFS

by Richard A. Fisher
Calvert Cliffs State Park

The cliffs formed over 15 million years ago, when all of southern Maryland was covered by a warm, shallow sea. As marine creatures died, they fell to the bottom of the sea, where they were covered and preserved in many layers of sediment.

When the last great ice sheets receded, there was a period of uplift in the land. The sea level fell to its present level, and the bottom of this shallow sea was exposed. The ancient seafloor is now being carved by the wind and waves—erosion—into the scenic cliffs we see today.

Over 600 species of fossil life have been identified in the cliffs. Most abundant are various species of shark, along with shells from phylum Mollusca (oysters, clams, etc.).

Today, visitors can take a 2-mile hike from the parking lot, along an improved trail to the cliffs at the beach. Natural wave action brings the fossils onto the beach, where they can be collected and kept.

CALVERT MARINE MUSEUM

This wonderful museum houses a terrific cross section of fossils big and small found in the region. Among the more enormous is an astonishing restoration of *Carcharocles megalodon*, a prehistoric shark. But there are many displays at the museum. And the Calvert Marine Museum Fossil Club offers outings too awesome to miss.

PO Box 97

Solomons, MD 20688

(410) 326-2042

Web site: http://www.calvertmarinemuseum.com/
  paleontology.htm

E-mail: mccormmj@co.cal.md.us

MARYLAND GEOLOGICAL SURVEY
2300 ST. PAUL ST.
BALTIMORE, MD 21218
(410) 554-5500
WEB SITE: HTTP://WWW.MGS.MD.GOV
E-MAIL: WWW@MGS.MD.GOV

Diplodocus

MASSACHUSETTS

AMHERST COLLEGE MUSEUM OF NATURAL HISTORY

Formerly the Pratt Museum of Natural History (which closed in March 2004), the museum reopened in 2006 as the Amherst College Museum of Natural History. The museum's Hall of Vertebrates is a wonderful example of evolutionary research. Early amphibians like *Eryops* and the sail-backed *Edaphosaurus,* along with prehistoric fish, set the stage for—*yes!*—DINOSAURS. A full mount of hadrosaur *Kritosaurus* from Alberta, Canada, is 12 feet tall. There are also skulls of *Tyrannosaurus rex* and *Triceratops,* as well as fossil pieces of the sauropod *Diplodocus* and dinosaur tracks.

> Amherst College
> Amherst, MA 01002
> (413) 542-2165
> Web site: http://www.amherst.edu/~pratt
> E-mail: sasauter@amherst.edu (Steve Sauter,
>   coordinator of education)

MUSEUM OF SCIENCE

Dan LoRusso is a wonderful dinosaur sculptor and scientist, and his recently created *Tyrannosaurus rex* model, or "6-ton canary," is part of the museum's renovated dinosaur exhibit. A *T. rex* timeline on the museum's Web site reveals how a *T. rex* model is created, one painstaking step at a time.

> Science Park
> Boston, MA 02114
> (617) 723-2500
> Web site: http://www.mos.org
> E-mail: information@mos.org

HARVARD MUSEUM OF NATURAL HISTORY

Hatching the Past: Dinosaur Eggs, Nests, and Young is one of the most amazing dinosaur exhibits at the Harvard Museum of Natural History. Modeled around "Baby Louie," a dinosaur embryo from a giant relative of *Oviraptor,* and other baby dinosaurs and eggs found all over the world, it poses the questions: Were dinosaurs social? Did they care for their hatchlings? And what did their babies actually look like? Other fossil exhibits, including displays on *Dimetrodon* (a sail-backed creature that came before dinosaurs and is distantly related to mammals) and *Kronosaurus* (a gigantic seagoing pliosaur from the Cretaceous of Australia) and the world-famous *Latimeria chalumnae*—a 7-foot coelacanth fish once thought to be extinct that was later caught—are also featured.

26 Oxford St.
Cambridge, MA 02138
(617) 495-3045
Web site: http://www.hmnh.harvard.edu
E-mail: hmnh@oeb.harvard.edu

DINOSAUR FOOTPRINTS

If you click on the "Western Massachusetts" link on the Trustees of Reser-

BONE DIGGER BONUS

BUILDING A REX

(Courtesy of the Museum of Science in Boston)

Meet Dan LoRusso—the artisan who turned steel, foam, and clay into the museum's sleek, contemporary Tyrannosaurus rex.

When the Museum of Science needed to replace its twenty-eight-year-old T. rex *with a model that reflected current scientific theories, it was a match made in dinosaur heaven. Paleo-artist Dan LoRusso had always dreamed of sculpting a life-size tyrant king. He just needed to find a location big enough to accommodate one.*

Luckily, Dan and the museum were already connected. As a second grader, Dan gave up his milk and cookie money to help support the building of the museum's first T. rex *in the 1960s. As a boy, he spent many hours at the Museum of Science and at Harvard's Museum of Comparative Zoology, poring over fossils and imagining a time when such creatures roamed Earth.*

Today, Dan is the creative force behind The Dinosaur Studio, Inc., a Medford, Massachusetts, company that constructs high-quality dinosaur sculptures for museums worldwide. Dan began his career as an industrial model and mold maker. Sculpting dinosaurs was a side hobby—as was volunteering in the museum's dinosaurs exhibit, where Dan often displayed his artfully rendered and scientifically accurate models.

One day over five years ago, a museum visitor who happened to work for a toy company took a keen interest in Dan's work. Since then, Dan has been a major contributor to the toy line of Safari Limited of Miami, Florida. He is also responsible for half of the Battat line of dinosaur replicas available in the museum's store. His models of Pachyrhinosaurus *and* Chasmosaurus *are on display in the Royal Tyrrell Museum of Paleontology in Alberta, Canada, and the Museo del Ricon in Colorado, Mexico, respectively.*

vations Web site and scroll down to "Dinosaur Footprints," you'll find a short description of the *Eubrontes giganteus* trackway left behind 200 million years ago by a three-toed meat-eater. If you scroll over the dots on the map of western Massachusetts, you'll discover the trackway is north of Springfield on Route 5.

(Rte. 5, north from Springfield)

Holyoke, MA 01040

(978) 921-1944

Web site: http://www.thetrustees.org/index.cfm

E-mail: information@ttor.org

WISTARIAHURST MUSEUM

This Victorian home is more an opulent mansion than a dinosaur exhibit, but the dinosaur tracks preserved in its outdoor walkways make this a paleo-stop even non-dinophiles might enjoy. When William Skinner's daughter, Belle, decided to renovate the grounds, she selected a red flagstone that was covered in dinosaur tracks. We're glad she did, because she gave us one more little dino-destination in Massachusetts.

238 Cabot St.

Holyoke, MA 01040

(413) 322-5660

Web site: http://www.wistariahurst.org

E-mail: wistariahurst@ci.holyoke.ma.us

NASH DINO LAND

Though Carlton S. Nash passed away in 1997, his son, Cornell Nash, has stepped in to keep his father's Dino Land dream alive. And happily so. When Nash senior discovered a remarkable dinosaur footprint quarry in 1933, he bought the 2-acre parcel of land and opened Nash Dino Land in 1939. For more than fifty years, he shared his passion for fossils with tourists who frequented his attraction. School groups keep the dream alive—but just barely. So stop by the Nash family's trackway before it goes extinct, like the dinosaurs who left their footprints.

Rte. 116, Amherst Rd.

South Hadley, MA 01075

(413) 467-9566

Web site: http://www.roadsideamerica.com/attract/
   MASOUnash.html

E-mail: NA

SPRINGFIELD SCIENCE MUSEUM

Dinosaur Hall features an old-school replica/model of *Tyrannosaurus rex*—a pose and general tone drawn straight from the 1960s, rather than more contemporary dinosaur thinking. But it's a classic not to be missed if you're in Springfield.

220 State St.
Springfield, MA 01103
(413) 263-6800
Web site: NA
E-mail: NA

MASSACHUSETTS GEOLOGICAL SURVEY
EXECUTIVE OFFICE OF ENVIRONMENTAL AFFAIRS
100 CAMBRIDGE ST., STE. 900
BOSTON, MA 02114
(617) 626-1000
WEB SITE: HTTP://WWW.STATE.MA.US/ENVIR/EOEA.HTM
E-MAIL: ENV.INTERNET@STATE.MA.US

Deinonychus

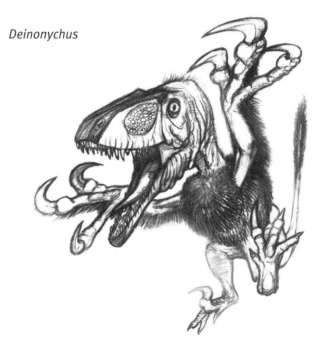

EXHIBIT MUSEUM OF NATURAL HISTORY

One of the museum's most impressive paleo-resources is its 220-million-year-old *Desmatosuchus* skeletal reconstruction and the two contrasting models that go with it. One, an aquatic model, was sculpted in 1930. The other model, more recently designed, is land bound, or terrestrial. It has not yet been determined which habitat was "home" to this crocodile-like prehistoric reptile found in Crosby County, Texas, in 1917 and 1919. You'll find the *Desmatosuchus* in the Hall of Evolution, along with 104 other exhibits that map out prehistoric life. *Deinonychus*, *Anchiceratops*, and *T. rex* are also represented.

> University of Michigan
> 1109 Geddes Ave.
> Ann Arbor, MI 48109
> (734) 764-0478
> Web site: http://www.exhibits.lsa.umich.edu/new/welcome.html
> E-mail: kiberman@umich.edu

KINGMAN MUSEUM OF NATURAL HISTORY

Three floors of interactive natural history exhibits include a display on the Ice Age in Michigan. There is also a replica of a *Protoceratops* nesting site and hatchling discovered by the legendary Roy Chapman Andrews, along with a *Protoceratops* skull and eggshells. Closed for a number of years, the renovated museum reopened in February 2003.

> 175 Limit St.
> Battle Creek, MI 49017
> (269) 965-5117
> Web site: http://www.kingmanmuseum.org
> E-mail: information@kingmanmuseum.org

CRANBROOK INSTITUTE OF SCIENCE

Our Dynamic Earth is a remarkable exhibit designed to profile the ever-changing face of life on Earth. Life Changes Over Time brings guests face to face with a full-size *T. rex* skeleton and a look at whether or not the giant reptile is related to modern-day birds. Ice Ages Come and Go examines Michigan during the Ice Age. Mastodons Did Not Survive explains why no mastodons survived extinction.

39221 Woodward Ave.
Bloomfield Hills, MI 48303
(877) 462-7262
Web site: http://science.cranbrook.edu
E-mail: form on Web site

BONE DIGGER BONUS

A ROY CHAPMAN ANDREWS LEGACY

by Robert Learner
Kingman Museum of Natural History

The Kingman Museum of Natural History's Protoceratops exhibit contains a replica of a nest—actual eggs and eggshells, a cast of a newly hatched baby—and the fossilized skull of an adult. These are from a 1922 Gobi Desert expedition led by Roy Chapman Andrews of the American Museum of Natural History, which confirmed that dinosaurs did, indeed, lay eggs.

The Protoceratops exhibition is one part of our Walk in the Footsteps of Dinosaurs exhibit. Here, visitors discover a one-tenth-scale habitat diorama of a dinosaur environ- ment, featuring five Jonas replicas; the fossilized, mounted complete leg of a Diplodocus; an exhibit of modern animals that lived during the time of the dinosaurs; and three "dinosaur digs," where children can find replicas of bones and then identify them using a large key on the wall.

Author's Note: What is a Jonas replica? It's a model or copy of a dinosaur created by the late Paul Jonas of New York. Although Jonas replicas are not up to current scientific thinking on dinosaur behavior, they are admired as art pieces. Jonas models are displayed in such well-known museums as the Smithsonian Institution's National Museum of Natural History and at the dinosaur trackways in Glen Rose, Texas.

Diplodocus

PUBLIC MUSEUM OF GRAND RAPIDS

The Web site not only leads to the Public Museum of Grand Rapids—it offers you a taste of the fossil finds you'll see there. It is a terrific cyber-preview of a collection that includes everything from fossil plants and *Allosaurus* to oreodonts and ancient amber (like that seen in *Jurassic Park*).

272 Pearl St. NW

Grand Rapids, MI 49504

(616) 456-3977

Web site: http://www.grmuseum.org/exhibits/a_to_z/fossils
   index.shtml

E-mail: tmawhinn@ci.grand-rapids.mi.us

KALAMAZOO VALLEY MUSEUM

Though there are some fossils in the Kalamazoo Valley Museum collection, they aren't on full-time exhibit, so you'll have to check periodically to see if they'll be on display when you want to visit. But the museum's permanent Mystery of the Mummy exploration of just how Egyptian mummies were preserved and later discovered by explorers is a terrific adventure. And the museum hosts special dinosaur exhibits on a regular basis.

230 N. Rose St.

Kalamazoo, MI 49003

(800) 772-3370

(269) 373-7990

Web site: http://kvm.kvcc.edu

E-mail: museumstaff@kvcc.edu

MICHIGAN BASIN GEOLOGICAL SOCIETY
PO BOX 18074
LANSING, MI 48901
(517) 241-3769
WEB SITE: HTTP://WWW.MBGS.ORG
E-MAIL: INFO@MBGS.ORG

Oreodont

MINNESOTA

NIAGARA CAVE

Nearly 400 million years ago, these caves began to form through a long and complicated geologic process. Today, they represent one of Minnesota's most amazing tourist stops. Within the caves mineralized formations contain fossils from life-forms that predate the dinosaurs. "There are several species of marine fossils embedded in the walls of Niagara Cave that visitors get an opportunity to view on the tour," according to Mark Bishop, who heads up the tour team. "*Receptaculites* (an algae that grew like a lily pad), cephalopods, gastropods, horn corals, and a trilobite. We also have a fossil display in our waiting area, which contains many more local varieties." No dinosaurs, but a winner just the same.

> (Hwy. 139 to County 30 west)
> PO Box 444
> Harmony, MN 55939
> (800) 837-6606
> Web site: http://www.niagaracave.com
> E-mail: niagara@means.net

SCIENCE MUSEUM OF MINNESOTA

Paleontology has been a primary focus of this museum since it was founded in 1907. Today, the museum is Minnesota's repository, charged with protecting and exhibiting the state's fossil treasures. Special attention has gone into studying ancient crocodilians and champsosaurs, as well as prehistoric turtles. The museum also carefully prepared When the Dinosaurs Were Gone, a traveling exhibit sponsored by the National Science Foundation. Many remarkable dinosaur specimens are on display, including *Camptosaurus, Haplocanthosaurus, Torosaurus, Diplodocus,* and *Triceratops*.

> 120 W. Kellogg Blvd.
> St. Paul, MN 55102
> (800) 221-9444
> (651) 221-9444
> Web site: http://www.smm.org
> E-mail: info@smm.org

Majungatholus

84

BONE DIGGER BONUS

DINOSAUR-EAT-DINOSAUR WORLD

(Courtesy of the Science Museum of Minnesota)

Macalester College geologist Ray Rogers and his wife, Science Museum of Minnesota pale-ontology curator Kristi Curry Rogers, joined colleague David Krause to publish the first con-firmed evidence of cannibalistic behavior among dinosaurs in the April 3, 2003, issue of Nature, *one of the most respected science journals in the world.*

Evidence gleaned from close examination of the fossilized bones of Majungatholus atopus, *a 30-foot-long meat-eating dinosaur that lived in Madagascar 65 to 70 million years ago, shows the* Majungatholus's *own distinctive tooth marks clearly imprinted on* Majungatholus *bones. The research also showed that* Majungatholus *was not exclusively cannibalistic: it also fed upon the remains of other dinosaurs, including long-necked sauropods called titanosaurs.*

According to Rogers, the fossil evidence is compelling and unprecedented—"We have examined literally thousands of dinosaur bones from sites around the world, and we've never seen fossil material quite like this." Fossilized bones from two Majungatholus *individ-uals indicate intense feeding, with distinctive sets of tooth marks that match the size and spacing of teeth in* Majungatholus's *jaws, and smaller grooves that match the sharp serra-tions on* Majungatholus's *bladelike teeth.*

Rogers and his colleagues are also careful to rule out other potential suspects who lived alongside Majungatholus. *"We examined the jaws and teeth of other known meat-eaters in the Malagasy fauna, including a much smaller carnivorous dinosaur called* Masiakasaurus knopfleri *(recently named after rock star Mark Knopfler [of the band Dire Straits]), and two large crocodiles," states Rogers, "but only* Majungatholus *possessed the jaws and teeth capable of inflicting the damage we see."*

While this is the first documented case of cannibalism among dinosaurs, the researchers feel that this discovery of cannibalism in a theropod dinosaur should come as no big surprise. Cannibalism as a feeding strategy is very common in the animal kingdom today. Animals ranging from insects to lions regularly consume members of their own species for a variety of ecologic and evolutionary reasons.

MINNESOTA GEOLOGICAL SURVEY
2642 UNIVERSITY AVE. W.
ST. PAUL, MN 55114
(612) 627-4780
WEB SITE: HTTP://WWW.GEO.UMN.EDU/MGS
E-MAIL: MGS@TC.UMN.EDU

MISSISSIPPI

W. M. BROWNING CRETACEOUS FOSSIL PARK

Booneville High School students were given a National Science Foundation grant and made the *ABC Evening News* in April and June 1991 after they discovered and collected hundreds of Cretaceous fossils along the construction site of Mississippi's Highway 45 bypass. Set down 75 million years ago, when the region was under the Demopolis Sea, the diversity of discovery was amazing: teeth from *Scapanorhynchus* and *Squalicorax,* two vicious prehistoric sharks; teeth from ancient fish *Enchodus* and *Xiphactinus;* teeth from mosasaurs, crocodiles, and even dinosaurs. It's a great and rare stop for scientists and fossil fans alike.

> Booneville Area Chamber of Commerce
>
> PO Box 927
>
> 100 W. Church St.
>
> Booneville, MS 38829
>
> (800) 300-9302
>
> (662) 728-4130
>
> Web site: http://www.boonevillemississippi.com/
>   recreation/fossil.htm
>
> E-mail: form on Web site

MISSISSIPPI PETRIFIED FOREST

Discovered in the mid-1800s, this petrified forest has only been open for public exploration for the past thirty years. A six-block nature trail with printed points-of-interest guides makes it easy to see and understand significant examples of prehistoric plant-life evidence. Named a registered national landmark by the National Park Service in 1966, it's a great outdoor glimpse of 36 million years of Mississippi's geologic past. Don't miss the great fossil display case in the gift shop and visitors center.

> PO Box 37
>
> 124 Forest Park Rd.
>
> Flora, MS 39071
>
> (601) 879-8189
>
> Web site: http://www.mspetrifiedforest.com
>
> E-mail: info@MSPetrifiedForest.com

MISSISSIPPI MUSEUM OF NATURAL SCIENCE

According to an MMNS newsletter, "Even though Mississippi was mostly covered with seawater during the Cretaceous Period, dinosaurs probably roamed the shoreline and inhabited nearby tropical islands." The museum's Stories in Stone exhibit beautifully showcases a great cross section of fossils, including those beachcombing dinosaurs and "Ziggy," its prized 15-foot *Zygorhiza* specimen (a prehistoric whale). Mississippi's Extinct Species exhibit takes a look at the plants and animals lost in recent centuries, due mostly to human destruction.

> 2148 Riverside Dr.
> Jackson, MS 39202
> (601) 354-7303
> Web site: http://www.mdwfp.com/museum
> E-mail: NA

BONE DIGGER BONUS

FOSSIL HIGH SCHOOL ROCKS

Imagine collecting fossils from an ancient ocean for high school science credit and you'll have a vague idea of what the faculty of Booneville High School in Mississippi pulled off, thanks to a grant from the National Science Foundation SGER (Small Grants for Exploratory Research).

When highway construction crews discovered a wealth of fossils in Frankstown's hills (south of Twenty Mile Creek), paleontology fans came running. Extinct shark teeth and jaws from Scapanorhynchus, *as well as an oyster bed and more, were almost immediately identified in the thick sand.*

Experts confirmed the fossils were from the Cretaceous of Mississippi, nearly 75 million years ago. Dagger-like teeth from the shark dazzled amateurs and experts. Extinct fish, such as Enchodus *and* Xiphactinus, *turtles, mosasaurs, crocodiles, and even dinosaur bits and pieces (hadrosaur teeth) also started to turn up.*

According to the local chamber of commerce, ABC News *was so impressed with the creative science skills of Booneville High School, they covered the story on the nightly news in April and June 1991.*

Fossils are still common in the area—so common that the W. M. Browning Cretaceous Fossil Park has been created to celebrate and protect the natural resources, a tribute to the prehistoric Demopolis Sea.

DUNN-SEILER MUSEUM

This university teaching museum has a proud and long history. Its collection was started in the late 1800s, before there was space dedicated for display. In June 1946, the board of trustees passed a resolution to create a museum in memory of geology student and instructor Franklin Carl Seiler, who was killed in action in World War II. Dr. Paul Heaney Dunn's name was added to the museum name after he devoted nearly thirty years to the department and the museum. Within the collection is a stunning *Triceratops* skull, a Cretaceous crocodile, and the beautifully preserved shell of a Cretaceous sea turtle, as well as prehistoric meteorites and other regional fossils.

Mississippi State University Department of Geosciences
Hilbun Hall
PO Box 5448
Mississippi State, MS 39762
(662) 325-3915
Web site: http://www.msstate.edu/dept/geosciences/
    4site/museum.htm
E-mail: cindy@geosci.msstate.edu

Triceratops

MISSISSIPPI DEPARTMENT
OF ENVIRONMENTAL QUALITY
OFFICE OF GEOLOGY
PO BOX 20307
JACKSON, MS 39289
(601) 961-5500
WEB SITE: HTTP://WWW.DEQ.STATE.MS.US
E-MAIL: CRAGIN_KNOX@DEQ.STATE.MS.US
(S. CRAGIN KNOX, STATE GEOLOGIST)

MISSOURI

MASTODON STATE HISTORIC SITE

Until archaeologists found a spearhead made by hunters of the Clovis culture firmly imbedded in the side of a fossilized mastodon at the Mastodon State Historic Site in 1979, there was no real proof man and mastodon had ever coexisted. Today, the historic site stands as a monument to that discovery and others made by archaeologists and paleontologists for more than 200 years. A full-size mastodon replica stands within the on-site museum, alongside other artifacts and fossils from the region. It's a terrific fossil stop you won't want to miss.

Department of Natural Resources
1050 Museum Dr.
Imperial, MO 63052
(800) 334-6946
(636) 464-2976
Web site: http://www.mostateparks.com/mastodon.htm
E-mail: moparks@dnr.mo.gov

EASTERN MISSOURI SOCIETY FOR PALEONTOLOGY

If you're looking to get dirty—and thrilled—in the space of an afternoon, don't miss studying this Web site before you head for St. Louis. The Eastern

Missouri Society for Paleontology has put together a *very* impressive list of ten places the average Joe can search for (and keep) certain very common fossils. But it's important to remember that all fossils on federal lands—lands not owned by private citizens—belong to all Americans. Fossils collected on federal land must be turned in to a repository or clearinghouse designated by the government.

PO Box 220273
St. Louis, MO 63122
Web site: http://www.mofossils.com/fossilsites.html
E-mail: paleophile@locustcreek.com

BONE DIGGER BONUS

MASTODON AND MAN

by Dr. Russ Graham
Mastodon State Park

Prehistorians and historians often feel like Sherlock Holmes, sleuthing through the foggy records of the past in order to reconstruct events and place them in perspective. Prehistoric sites are like crime scenes without witnesses. These investigations depend upon physical evidence—biological remains—like fossils, bones, teeth, plant parts, shells, and so on, buried in the earth.

Historians and prehistorians are frequently drawn into their work by the sense of discovery. I have enjoyed the pursuit at the Kimmswick site and bone beds located about 20 miles south of St. Louis at Mastodon State Park. Fossils of extinct Ice Age mammals, especially mastodons, have been found at this site since the early nineteenth century.

A variety of private excavations occurred at the site until the early 1940s. One important event has been documented. Stone artifacts were found (circa 1907) with the bones of these extinct animals (suggesting that early man coexisted with prehistoric giants). The artifacts have been preserved at the Field Museum in Chicago, Illinois. This was one of the first times this association between man and beast was demonstrated in North America. But because the find was not scientifically documented, it was not generally accepted—and rightly so—by the scientific community.

In 1979, I led excavations at Kimmswick. These excavations provided conclusive evidence that humans were associated with the extinct mastodons. Stone spearpoints and other stone artifacts were found with the bones of these and other animals. I am now researching the evidence. These studies should answer such questions as "What were the prehistoric people doing at Kimmswick?" and "What was the relationship between the people and the prehistoric animals?"

It has been fun for me to conduct inquiries into the past events of Kimmswick. But I can't help but wonder—how might Sherlock Holmes have approached this investigation?

ST. LOUIS SCIENCE CENTER/DINOSAUR PARK

Though there are no permanent dinosaur exhibits inside the St. Louis Science Center, there is a collection of dinosaur models called a Dinosaur Park outside the center in the St. Louis Forest Park, including *Triceratops* and *Tyrannosaurus rex*. And to the Science Center's credit, it has featured some very creative dinosaur exhibits in the past, including a cooperative fossil-prep lab staffed by members of the Eastern Missouri Society for Paleontology.

> 5050 Oakland Ave.
> St. Louis, MO 63110
> (800) 456-7572
> (314) 289-4444
> Web site: http://www.slsc.org
> E-mail: webmaster@slsc.org

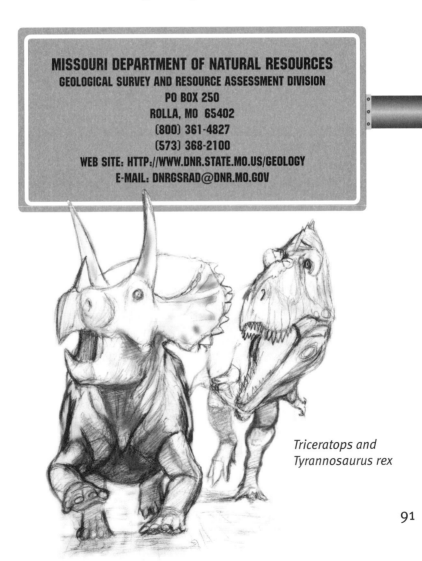

MISSOURI DEPARTMENT OF NATURAL RESOURCES
GEOLOGICAL SURVEY AND RESOURCE ASSESSMENT DIVISION
PO BOX 250
ROLLA, MO 65402
(800) 361-4827
(573) 368-2100
WEB SITE: HTTP://WWW.DNR.STATE.MO.US/GEOLOGY
E-MAIL: DNRGSRAD@DNR.MO.GOV

Triceratops and Tyrannosaurus rex

MONTANA

MUSEUM OF THE ROCKIES

Jurassic Park advisor Dr. John R. "Jack" Horner is the heart and soul of this wonderful museum in the heart of Big Sky Country. Dr. Horner first made a paleo-splash when he discovered "Egg Mountain" and the fossil evidence that *Maiasaura* nested collectively and cared for their young. Today, he and his museum associates have gone on to tackle in-depth studies of *Tyrannosaurus rex* as a scavenger rather than a hunter, dinosaur DNA, sauropod nesting grounds, and much more. Visiting his home museum and the university that sponsors it is a must for dinophiles visiting Montana. And if you're prone to real-life paleontology experiences, sign up for the museum's hands-on field programs. Dig alongside the best of the best in a world-famous dinosaur setting.

600 W. Kagy Blvd.

Bozeman, MT 59717

(406) 994-2251

Web site: http://www.montana.edu/wwwmor

E-mail: wwwmor@montana.edu

TREX AGATE SHOP

If you wander through Bynum, Montana, and find Marion Brandvold's famous rock shop is closed, it might be wise to check back in the very near future. Nine times out of ten, if the avid fossil fan is out of the store, she's out in the field, scoping out dinos. Her most famous discovery? The tiny *Maiasaura* hatchling that led paleontologist Jack Horner to "Egg Mountain" and the "good mother" dinosaur nesting ground. Tiny bones scattered across a hot, sandy hillside caught her eye. Once her son had pieced them together, the whole Brandvold family knew what they had discovered—a baby dinosaur. So be patient if the Trex Agate Shop is closed when you arrive. You never know what Marion will find on her next Big Sky outdoor walkabout.

161 S. Front St.

PO Box 796

Bynum, MT 59419

(406) 469-2314

Web site: http://www.trexagateshop.com

E-mail: trex@3rivers.net

Maiasaura

OLD TRAIL MUSEUM

For around $200, plus transportation, you can join Old Trail Museum curator of paleontology Todd Crowell on a two-day summer paleontology adventure in the region that produced Jack Horner's "Egg Mountain." If that's too rich for your blood (or too hot for your comfort zone), visit this lovely small-town museum instead. Dinosaur fossils are a big part of the museum's exhibits, and life-size dinosaur models "prowl" outside the museum grounds. But they aren't the only points of interest. Pulitzer Prize–winning novelist Bud Guthrie has an exhibit on-site. Poor "Old Sol," an arrowpoint-riddled human skeleton, is on display, a testament to the accuracy of Native American weaponry. And of course, grizzly bears are celebrated in an exhibit.

823 N. Main St.
Choteau, MT 59422
(406) 466-5332
Web site: NA
E-mail: otm@3rivers.net

BONE DIGGER BONUS

THE LEGENDARY "GOOD MOTHER" FIND

by Dr. Jack Horner
Museum of the Rockies

I was lucky enough to grow up in northern Montana, where conditions are just right for pre-serving and exposing fossils. Since I was very small, I have been fascinated by the fossils found in the badlands around my home. I have always seen dinosaurs a little differently from the way most people do, and my research tends to reflect that difference.

Instead of concentrating on finding new specimens, and lots of them, I want to know how they lived and be able to convey a more complete idea about the living, breathing, functional animals that these bones represent.

One aspect of my studies has dealt with Maiasaura. *Because of several sites in Montana, we have snapshots in time of how these animals lived. At the nesting grounds for these large animals, a range of sizes and developmental stages is preserved, which allows us to make inferences—educated guesses—about their growth rates, herding behaviors, and community interactions.*

Taking into account the environment in which they lived, we are also able to make estimations about the ecology of the total community of which these animals were a part.

PINE BUTTE SWAMP PRESERVE

Devoutly protected by the Nature Conservancy, this 18,000-acre parcel of land was actually purchased to guarantee the survival of one of the grizzly bear's last habitat strongholds. But nestled within that stretch of land is Jack Horner's famous bone bed, "Egg Mountain." Eighty million years ago, herds of migratory duckbilled dinosaurs nested in this ancient spot year after year after year. Generations of fossil evidence support that scenario, thanks to the dedication of Dr. Horner. Through a special agreement, he continues his research with the conservancy's blessing. Young people staying at the Pine Butte Guest Ranch even enjoy tours of the dig site.

(Hwy. 89)
Pine Butte Guest Ranch
HC58-Box 34 C
Choteau, MT 59422
(406) 466-2158
Web site: http://www.nature.org/wherewework/northamerica/
    states/montana/preserves/art342.html
E-mail: ebergman@tnc.org (Eric Bergman, naturalist and
    education coordinator)

CARTER COUNTY MUSEUM

Ekalaka is not a *big* Montana town. It's small and homey and not likely to give Los Angeles or New York a run for its hustle-bustle money anytime soon. But proudly thriving on one end of the town's modest Main Street is the Carter County Museum. Within the large space are some of the most beautiful dinosaur fossils on Earth, very humbly displayed. Little comes between the visitor and the authentic bones (as opposed to museum reproductions usually on display). The dark glow of the real bone has a distinct look to it—a shine you never forget. Along with a duckbill specimen and other scattered fossils, you'll see regional "wow" exhibits, including a two-headed calf!

306 N. Main St.
PO Box 547
Ekalaka, MT 59324
(406) 775-6886
Web site: http://www.cartercountymt.com/museum.htm
E-mail: NA

UPPER MUSSELSHELL HISTORICAL MUSEUM

In addition to being an 1800s-era schoolroom, this small museum features the skull of an *Avaceratops,* a horned dinosaur, found in the early 1980s at a nearby ranch. Various duckbill fossil parts are also on display.

11 S. Central Ave.
Harlowton, MT 59036
(406) 632-5519
Web site: http://www.ohwy.com/mt/u/upmussmu.htm
E-mail: NA

GARFIELD COUNTY MUSEUM

Jordan, Montana, is a dinosaur town. Folks have been picking prehistoric fossils up out of the dust there for as long as anyone can remember. This small museum respects that ancient heritage and puts it up on display. A fiberglass replica of a 6-ton *Triceratops* found in 1965, 25 miles north of Jordan, is on view, as is a duckbilled *Edmontosaurus* skull and a *T. rex* skull, also found by locals. There is also a 1912-era schoolhouse and a blacksmith shop reconstructed as part of the museum's exhibits.

(Hwy. 200, between Jordan and Circle)

PO Box 325

Jordan, MT 59337

(406) 557-2517

Web site: http://www.garfieldcounty.com

E-mail: chamber@garfieldcounty.com (Garfield County
   Chamber of Commerce)

JUDITH RIVER DINOSAUR INSTITUTE

What started as a small-town, northern Montana museum jumped to become a first-class dinosaur museum, thanks to paleontologist Nate Murphy and the discovery of "Leonardo," the most complete dinosaur ever discovered, according to the *Guinness Book of World Records*. Leonardo was mummified before he was fossilized. As a result, much of his soft tissue—skin, muscle, internal organs,

Edmontosaurus

95

ornamental frills, and even his stomach contents—was fossilized along with his skeleton. Leonardo is on display along with many other dinosaur discoveries made by Murphy and the Judith River Dinosaur Institute. And volunteer digs are offered for a fee three times a year in the summer months, so you can help make the next discovery.

PO Box 429

Malta, MT 59538

(406) 654-2323

Web site: http://www.montanadinosaurdigs.com

E-mail: nmurphy@ttc-cmc.net

MUSSELSHELL VALLEY HISTORICAL MUSEUM

Opened in 1972, this all-around regional history museum is 7,000 square feet of bits and pieces, revealing nineteenth-century life from blacksmiths to newspapers to switchboards. But part of the collection is an extensive rock and fossil display. Considering that this part of Montana is pretty dinosaur-rich, many of the fossils represent dinosaur treasure. While there may not be a lot in terms of fossil adventure, this museum is unlikely to leave you disappointed.

524 First St. W.

Roundup, MT 59072

(406) 323-1403

Web site: http://www.mvhm.us

E-mail: NA

MONTANA BUREAU OF MINES AND GEOLOGY
1300 W. PARK ST.
BUTTE, MT 59701
(406) 496-4167
WEB SITE: HTTP://WWW.MBMG.MTECH.EDU
E-MAIL: NFAVERO@MTECH.EDU

THE ELEANOR BARBOUR COOK MUSEUM OF GEOLOGY

Named for the academic daughter of celebrated Nebraska paleontologist E. H. Barbour, the Eleanor Barbour Cook Museum of Geology is a tribute both to paleontology and to Eleanor's sheer determination. Conceived in 1938, the museum's early collection was devoted to geoscience, with 637 invertebrate fossils, 700 minerals, 284 modern shells and coral, 111 mounted birds, and 19 mounted mammals. Many scientists from the region helped the collection grow, until Mrs. Cook retired in 1941. Without supervision, many of the specimens were lost. The museum rallied in the 1970s under the watch of Larry Agenbroad and two other devoted experts. Today, Dr. Mike Leite respectfully stewards the museum as Eleanor Barbour Cook no doubt intended. Be sure to check out "Mr. T," a partial skull of a *Triceratops* collected by Chadron State College geoscience students near Lusk, Wyoming.

> Chadron State College
> 1000 Main St.
> Chadron, NE 69337
> (800) 242-3766
> Web site: http://www.csc.edu/geoscience/museum0.htm
> E-mail: inquire@csc.edu

HUDSON-MENG BISON BONEBED

Ranger Albert Meng knew he'd stumbled upon something remarkable when he discovered a cache of fossilized bones tumbling from an eroding soil bank more than fifty years ago. But it took years for him and his friend Bill Hudson to get any experts to take a look. When Dr. Larry Agenbroad finally led a professional excavation in the 1970s, it was clear that something catastrophic had wiped out hundreds of prehistoric bison. But what had caused the carnage? Stone artifacts found near the bone bed suggest prehistoric man might have been the culprit. Paleontological and archaeological experts come from all over the world to study and theorize about the mystery, even today. When you visit Nebraska, maybe you can do the same.

> Nebraska National Forest
> 125 N. Main St.
> Chadron, NE 69337
> (308) 432-0300
> Web site: http://www.fs.fed.us/r2/nebraska/units/prrd/
>   hm/hudsonmeng.html
> E-mail: NA

TRAILSIDE MUSEUM OF NATURAL HISTORY

Giant mammoths, fossil rhinos, and a giant tortoise are the prehistoric jewels in this small university museum's collection. But all of Nebraska's geologic fossil history is touched upon in exhibits. School visits are available upon request, and the American West and Native American Art Gallery—an exhibit featuring the work of local artists—is also on-site.

Fort Robinson State Park

PO Box 462

Crawford, NE 69339

(308) 665-2929

Web site: http://www.museum.unl.edu/trailside

E-mail: NA

AGATE FOSSIL BEDS NATIONAL MONUMENT

Hundreds of Miocene animals, including the two-horned rhino *Menoceras* and a clawed but otherwise horselike creature called *Moropus,* met with a mysterious end 19.2 million years ago. Today, teams of paleontologists work to recover their fossilized remains and secrets at the Agate Fossil Beds National Monument—3,000 acres of preserved land and a monument to former land owner "Captain" James H. Cook. Cook's ranch was also a gathering place for the Oglala Lakota Sioux.

301 River Rd.

Harrison, NE 69346

(308) 668-2211

Web site: http://www.nps.gov/agfo

E-mail: form on Web site

WILDLIFE WORLD AT WYOBRASKA NATURAL HISTORY MUSEUM

Museum literature says the museum features fossils, dioramas, and over 300 animal specimens from six continents, all in a renovated train station. And there's no doubt the collection is impressive and the building is lovely, from an adult point of view. But if you're a kid looking for that final "something" to convince you Wildlife World is worth the fossil stop, I've got one word for you: *Baluchitherium* (now known as *Indricotherium*). This stunning replica of an oddly horselike rhino is a whopping 19 feet tall and more than 30 feet long. It's a giant among prehistoric giants, and well worth the time it takes to see it. Other fossils are on display in the museum, including *Triceratops*. But this mammalian Goliath is the museum's real star.

950 U St.

Gering, NE 69341

(308) 436-7104
Web site: http://www.wyobraskawildlifemuseum.com
E-mail: NA

UNIVERSITY OF NEBRASKA STATE MUSEUM

Nebraska's prehistoric fish fossils are amazing. And the dark and mysterious Mesozoic Gallery at the University of Nebraska State Museum deftly displays numerous large marine fossils in 750 square feet of exhibit space. Even the floor space is creatively utilized to exhibit the fossil fish in an incredibly dramatic and striking backlit fashion. Interactive computer displays and touch maps that reveal the shifting prehistoric continents help explain the fossils you see. As if that weren't enough, the museum's world-famous collection of prehistoric elephants in Elephant Hall, the fossil rhinos and horses, and the fossil discovery touch-and-learn exhibits round out the museum's impressive prehistoric offerings. This is a world-class museum you'll be glad you explored.

307 Morrill Hall
University of Nebraska—Lincoln
Lincoln, NE 68588
(402) 472-2642
Web site: http://www.museum.unl.edu
E-mail: afox1@unl.edu (Angie Fox)

BONE DIGGER BONUS

DR. MICHAEL R. VOORHIES REMEMBERS

by Dr. Michael R. Voorhies
Formerly of the University of Nebraska State Museum

I grew up in a small town in northeastern Nebraska and became fascinated by the fossilized mammal teeth I found on the sandbars of the cool, clear streams near home. Some people grow out of their early love for fossils, but I never did.

I studied geology at the University of Nebraska and worked for the State Museum in the summer, helping add to its enormous collection of fossil elephants, camels, rhinos, and oreodonts. Later, I was lucky enough to work with Morris Skinner, the greatest bone hunter who ever prowled the canyons of northeastern Nebraska.

The most exciting fossil deposit I've ever investigated is the volcanic ash bed at Ashfall Fossil Beds. It's like a prehistoric moment frozen in time.

ASHFALL FOSSIL BEDS STATE HISTORICAL PARK

Herds of prehistoric mammals once gathered at a watering hole some 10 million years ago. As rhinos, three-toed horses, camels, and other species drank the cool water, a volcano violently erupted, trapping them beneath the lava and the ash. Frozen in their death poses, they were discovered by scientists in the 1970s. Excavation continues today.

86930 517th Ave.

Royal, NE 68773

(402) 893-2000

Web site: http://www.ashfall.unl.edu

E-mail: ashfall2@unl.edu

CONSERVATION AND SURVEY DIVISION
SCHOOL OF NATURAL RESOURCES
102 NEBRASKA HALL
UNIVERSITY OF NEBRASKA—LINCOLN
LINCOLN, NE 68588
(402) 472-3471
WEB SITE: HTTP://CSD.UNL.EDU
E-MAIL: SNRSALES@UNL.EDU

NEVADA

BERLIN-ICHTHYOSAUR STATE PARK

Ichthyosaurs were ancient marine reptiles that swam in the warm oceans that covered much of the Earth 225 million years ago. Nevada's ichthyosaur, a species known as *Shonisaurus popularis,* was as much as 50 feet long—a giant in the waters. Ichthyosaurs were found all over the world, and fossil evidence indicates that at least some of these animals gave birth to live young, though they were reptiles and not marine mammals like dolphins. Fossils are

BONE DIGGER BONUS

PREHISTORIC WILD THINGS AT BERLIN-ICHTHYOSAUR STATE PARK

(Courtesy of the Nevada Commission on Tourism)

If the phantasmic creatures depicted in Jurassic Park *and* The Lost World *stimulated your interest in prehistoric fauna, consider a trip to Berlin-Ichthyosaur State Park, built around the fossilized remains of ancient, mysterious reptiles and a well-preserved turn-of-the-century Nevada mining camp.*

The ichthyosaur Shonisaurus popularis *was a swimming carnivore, 50 to 60 feet long, averaging some 40 tons. Its body was shaped much like a whale, and its head was about 10 feet long, set with eyeballs a foot across. It had a long, narrow snout full of pointed teeth designed for ripping flesh. Kind of like a gigantic bottle-nosed dolphin with a bad attitude.*

It is probably safe to assume that such an animal ruled the warm, shallow seas that covered Nevada during the Late Triassic Period, when dinosaurs first appeared. (The Jurassic Period, the second period in the Age of Dinosaurs, followed.)

Shonisaurus was an ichthyosaur, a reptile that bore its young alive, and is not closely related to any living reptiles. "Big Icky" became extinct millions of years ago—scientists disagree about just when—but the reasons for the species' demise are unclear.

These sea beasts came to rest in an area that today is a mountain canyon, well above the timberline. During their time, between 230 and 220 million years ago, Nevada was flat, the bed of a receding sea linked to the Pacific Ocean. The ichthyosaurs were buried shortly after death under what is now sedimentary rock.

Later, the land began to crack and shift, lifting up in spots to form the north-south mountain ranges that exist today. As those mountains eroded, the fossilized bones of the long-dead creatures re-emerged on the side of a mountain in what by then was known as Union Canyon in the Shoshone Mountain Range of Nevada.

The Nevada ichthyosaurs were first discovered in 1928 by Dr. S. M. Muller of Stanford University. However, Berlin old-timers recalled that during the mining camp's heyday, the area was peppered with small fossils and other reminders of the area's prehistoric past.

It wasn't until 1954 that any serious excavation of the site began. That was when Dr. Charles Camp of the University of California at Berkeley, assisted by Dr. Sam Welles and a squad of student volunteers, uncovered six ichthyosaurs. Thirty-four have since been found, and visitors today can see an exhibit of nine or ten of the best specimens.

Ichthyosaurs have been discovered on every continent except possibly Antarctica. Nevada's Shonisaurus popularis is nearly the largest ichthyosaur ever found, second only to a newly discovered species from British Columbia (Canada). This is one of the reasons why Shonisaurus is Nevada's official state fossil.

The fossil bed is today covered by a big A-frame shed, which is opened for tours by the resident ranger at 10 a.m., 2 p.m., and 4 p.m. weekdays from Memorial Day through Labor Day, and at 10 a.m. and 2 p.m. weekends from Labor Day to mid-November. Specially arranged tours are possible by appointment.

on display at the park's Fossil House. You'll find the park 23 miles east of Gabbs, via State Route 844.

HC 61, Box 61200

Austin, NV 89310

(775) 964-2440

Web site: http://www.parks.nv.gov/bi.htm

E-mail: region3@cccomm.net

LAS VEGAS NATURAL HISTORY MUSEUM

If you're looking for Las Vegas dinosaurs, this is the place to go. From the Dinosaur Den to the Young Scientists Center, there are fossil finds all around. Robotic dinosaurs, including *Tyrannosaurus rex, Triceratops,* raptors, and a mother dinosaur with hatchlings, delight dinosaur fans of all ages. Prehistoric mammals, including a four-tusked elephant, a 52-foot-long ancient crocodile, and a saber-toothed cat, are also on display. Perhaps most relevant to Nevada, though, is the ichthyosaur exhibit. The marine reptiles thrived in the ancient sea that covered Nevada during the day of the dinosaur. Smaller fossil fans will love the Young Scientist Center with its Dig-a-Fossil area, Rub-a-Dino Paleontologist Lab, and a robotic baby dinosaur children can operate.

900 N. Las Vegas Blvd.

Las Vegas, NV 89101

(702) 384-3466

Web site: http://www.lvnhm.org

E-mail: dino@vnhm.org

Triceratops baby

MARJORIE BARRICK MUSEUM OF NATURAL HISTORY

A very modest display of fossils is on exhibit at this elegant museum of natural history, along with extensive contemporary insect and animal specimens.

4505 S. Maryland Pkwy.

Las Vegas, NV 89154

(702) 895-3381

Web site: http://hrc.nevada.edu/museum

E-mail: gigueta@unlv.nevada.edu

W. M. KECK EARTH SCIENCE AND MINERAL ENGINEERING MUSEUM

Stunning photos of fossils exhibited in the university's geology museum are on display at the Web site—ammonites, brachiopods, mollusks, bryozoans, trilobites, and ichthyosaurs that thrived in an ancient prehistoric sea over Nevada. But the museum's history is almost as interesting as its collections. It opened in 1908 to help house the Mackay silver collection, and was renovated and reopened in 1988, after the W. M. Keck Foundation funded the ambitious project. Other minerals and mining artifacts are also on display, along with that Mackay silver collection.

University of Nevada, Reno

Mackay School of Mines Bldg.

1664 N. Virginia St.

Reno, NV 89557

(775) 784-4528

Web site: http://www.mines.unr.edu/museum

E-mail: rdolbier@unr.edu

GEOLOGICAL SOCIETY OF NEVADA
PO BOX 13375
RENO, NV 89507
(775) 323-3500
WEB SITE: HTTP://WWW.GSNV.ORG
E-MAIL: GSN@MINES.UNR.EDU

THE SARGENT MUSEUM OF ARCHAEOLOGY AND ANTHROPOLOGY

Although this is a museum of ancient sciences other than paleontology, it does offer a children's "Dino Detective" class in cooperation with the Children's Museum of Portsmouth, New Hampshire. Participants unearth a *Triceratops* skull replica, piece together a dinosaur puzzle, catalog replica fossils, and listen to dinosaur sounds. Call (603) 436-3853 for information.

> PO Box 4212
> Concord, NH 03302
> (603) 627-4802
> Web site: http://www.sargentmuseum.org
> E-mail: info@sargentmuseum.org

THE WOODMAN INSTITUTE

Before Annie Woodman "passed to a higher life" in 1915, she set aside $100,000 to create an educational museum. The Woodman Institute opened a year and six months later, in July 1916. Annie Woodman would be proud to know her dream still thrives today. A 10-foot-tall polar bear mount greets visitors as they enter this little-known "jewel of the seacoast" museum. And if they search with determination, and ask a few questions, they can also find a very limited fossil collection (along with a two-headed snake, a 27-pound lobster, and a four-legged chicken). There is even a saddle once owned by Abraham Lincoln on display. So what you don't find in fossils, you'll make up for in the bizarre.

> 182 Central Ave.
> Dover, NH 03820
> (603) 742-1038
> Web site: http://www.seacoastnh.com/woodman
> E-mail: NA

THE LITTLE NATURE MUSEUM

Director Sandra Martin is devoted to science, kids, and education. Her small but mighty nature center reflects that devotion. Classrooms and teachers can visit the center (by appointment) to study dinosaurs, rocks and minerals, insects, reptiles, seeds, the human body, and much more. It's a very personal, hands-on museum experience—truly one of a kind. Remember, it's by appointment only (spring through fall) so call, e-mail, or write to Ms. Martin in advance.

> Gould Hill Orchards
> 656 Gould Hill Rd.
> Contoocook, NH 03229
> (603) 746-6121
> Web site: http://www.littlenaturemuseum.org
> E-mail: nature-museum@conknet.com

BONE DIGGER BONUS

THE LITTLE MUSEUM THAT COULD

by Sandra Martin
Director of the Little Nature Museum

Author's Note: Ten years ago, Sandra Martin talked to me about the fossil resources at the Little Nature Museum for another dinosaur travel book I wrote. When it came time to write this guide, she reflected on what ten years have yielded.

The museum, in its forty-eighth year, still has its fossils—lots more, in fact, than ten years ago. We have one major nature trail on the Orchard property, as well as an outdoor discovery area for children in grades K through 3. The museum is run entirely by volunteers, including myself.

Over 1,000 visitors came to the museum from the end of August 2003 until it closed for the season at the end of October. We are letting visitors see the museum for free in the hopes of encouraging donations. The museum received its federal nonprofit status five years ago, which has opened a number of doors for us.

Dinosaurs and fossils continue to be programs that I regularly present to children. We have added many dinosaur reproductions (claws, brain replicas, etc.) from my travels, which have taken me to Dinosaur National Monument (I spent two days there), Dinosaur Provincial Park, and the Royal Tyrrell Museum.

I love dinosaurs, too, and enjoy collecting artifacts children can handle. I enjoy showing how paleontologists learn about dinosaurs from studying animals that live today. I use modern-day skulls to have children learn about what animals eat and then we look at drawings of dinosaur skulls to try to determine what they ate. It's great fun.

Diplodocus skull

NEW HAMPSHIRE DEPARTMENT OF ENVIRONMENTAL SERVICES
29 HAZEN DR.
PO BOX 95
CONCORD, NH 03302
(603) 271-3503
WEB SITE: HTTP://WWW.DES.STATE.NH.US
E-MAIL: FORM ON WEB SITE

NEW JERSEY

HADDONFIELD BRONZE HADROSAUR

In the summer of 1858, fossil hobbyist William Parker Foulke vacationed in Haddonfield, New Jersey. He'd heard a rumor that workers at a local marl pit had found gigantic bones of a mysterious animal, and he wanted to investigate the pit for himself. With the help of a dig team he did exactly that, unearthing the fossilized bones of an animal, later named *Hadrosaurus foulkii,* that seemed to be part elephant and part bird. It was the first reasonably complete dinosaur skeleton ever discovered. A bronze-and-stone marker at the site first commemorated the discovery. But the citizens of Haddonfield felt the first dinosaur ever unearthed deserved more than a stone marker. So they formed H.A.T.C.H.—Haddonfield Acts To Create *Hadrosaurus foulkii*. Their goal? To install a life-size bronze sculpture at the center of the town's business district and to claim their proud place in history. Sculptor John Giannotti was commissioned to create the bronze sculpture, and a fund-raising effort to pay the $100,000 in expenses went into full swing. H.A.T.C.H. sponsored parades and sold T-shirts, buttons, lapel pins—you name it—to help pay the bills. And in October 2003, their dream came true. So be sure to visit the Haddonfield hadrosaur if you're in the region.

(Lantern Ln. near Kings Hwy., Haddonfield, NJ)
Mailing address:
H.A.T.C.H. Dinosaur Committee
114 Kings Hwy. E.

Haddonfield, NJ 08033
(856) 429-4580
Web site: http://www.hadrosaurus.com and
    http://www.levins.com/dinosaur.shtml
E-mail: bevaldegh@comcast.net or HoagL@earthlink.net

BONE DIGGER BONUS

HADDONFIELD,
THE FIRST U.S. "DINOSAUR TOWN"

by Hoag Levins
Journalist and H.A.T.C.H. Volunteer

One thing the Hadrosaurus *sculpture installation will help to underscore is the little-appreciated fact that Haddonfield was America's first dinosaur town.*

Your book documents the country's "dinosaur towns"—those places that have witnessed significant paleontological discoveries or events that have become a part of their identity. Haddonfield, which is the place where the world's first relatively complete dinosaur skeleton was found, became the first dinosaur town for that reason.

Moreover, shortly after that discovery was made, Edward Drinker Cope moved his family to Haddonfield from Philadelphia in order to be closer to the marl fields of southern New Jersey that had become the hottest dinosaur-fossil hunting fields in North America. In 1866, Cope discovered the world's second reasonably complete dinosaur fossil at a marl pit 12 miles south of Haddonfield. It was also here in his home on the main street of Haddonfield that Cope entertained O. C. Marsh and took him on a tour of the surrounding marl fields in the opening weeks of 1869.

In fact, that two-week visit by Marsh with Cope in Haddonfield was the very beginning of what became the "Bone Wars." (Marsh later went back to offer money to all the marl pit operators to send him their fossils rather than Cope.) Cope, who used his barn as a fossil preparation site, ran the first decade of the Bone Wars from his Haddonfield home. He would travel west in the summer and spend the winters here, writing up his incredible flow of scientific papers.

The Hadrosaurus *sculpture is just one of the attractions here. The actual site at which the bones were originally excavated is now a wild stretch of parkland that looks much like it did in 1858. A small commemorative park is established there, and the town is in planning discussions with county and state agencies to establish larger educational facilities at the actual wooded excavation site. The preliminary plans call for boardwalks that span the river and swamp areas and allow visitors to easily and safely stand at the very spot where the human race first dug up the collection of fossil bones that showed what the anatomy of a dinosaur actually looked like.*

MORRIS MUSEUM

Morristown, New Jersey, is a town with serious history, and this museum proves it. Founded in 1913, the Morris was the first museum ever accredited by the American Association of Museums. More to the point of this book, however, many of the fossils on display in the Dinosaur and Fossils gallery were found close to home. The geology and paleontology collection is the museum's *biggest* collection—bigger than dolls and toys, bigger than anthropology, bigger than fine art. It's definitely worth a side trip to Morristown while dino-touring in New Jersey.

> 6 Normandy Heights Rd.
>
> Morristown, NJ 07960
>
> (973) 971-3700
>
> Web site: http://www.morrismuseum.org
>
> E-mail: information@morrismuseum.org

RUTGERS UNIVERSITY GEOLOGY MUSEUM

According to the Geology Museum's Web site, "The largest exhibits include a dinosaur trackway from Towaco, New Jersey; a mastodon from Salem County, New Jersey; and an Egyptian mummy." An Egyptian mummy? In a geology museum? Never mind. Wrap your mind around *Grallator*—the meat-eating dinosaur responsible for laying down nearly all of the tracks on display at this Jersey museum. Known only by its footprints—no fossilized bones have ever been found to go with them—it's been identified through comparative anatomy. Scientists compared *these* tracks to the feet of dinosaurs known from skeletons, and decided *Grallator* was a theropod about 8 feet long, much like *Coelophysis* from Arizona and New Mexico. The mastodon is one of 600 different kinds of prehistoric elephants found all over the world. New Jersey was "elephant country" 10,000 years ago, and this mastodon was found in 1869. The mummy is of a woman mummified 2,400 years ago in Egypt.

> Old Queens Section
>
> College Avenue Campus
>
> New Brunswick, NJ 08903
>
> (732) 932-7243
>
> Web site: http://geology.rutgers.edu/museum.html (museum
>   home page)
>
> E-mail: rwselden@rci.rutgers.edu (R. William Seblen)

THE BERGEN MUSEUM OF ART AND SCIENCE

Though primarily an art museum, the Bergen does exhibit two mastodons, one called the Hackensack mastodon (discovered in 1962 while a freeway was being carved out of the landscape), the other called the Dwarskill mastodon (excavated in 1973).

Bergen Mall

E. State Rte. 4 and Forest Ave.

Paramus, NJ 07652

(201) 291-8848

Web site: http://www.thebergenmuseum.com

E-mail: info@thebergenmuseum.com

JENKINSON'S AQUARIUM

Although this is a traditional aquarium featuring traditional, contemporary animals, it's also an educational outreach center for New Jersey teachers and citizens. A special fossil room reminds visitors there were marine creatures around before man's time on Earth began. And special workshops offer participants the chance to search for New Jersey fossils, make fossil replicas, and even compare living sharks to prehistoric relatives. It's a terrific resource for fossil fans with an oceanic flare.

300 Ocean Ave.

Pt. Pleasant Beach, NJ 08742

(732) 892-0600

Web site: http://www.jenkinsons.com/aquarium

E-mail: form on Web site

NEW JERSEY STATE MUSEUM

Until the town of Haddonfield started banging its dinosaur drum, it was a little-known fact that the first reasonably complete dinosaur ever discovered was found there in 1858. Scattered bones had been found in Europe and other parts of North America. But *Hadrosaurus foulkii* was the first dinosaur skeleton ever mounted and displayed in public. That hadrosaur, along with other aspects of New Jersey's prehistoric record—including Ice Age mastodons—is on display at this state museum.

205 W. State St.

Trenton, NJ 08608

(609) 292-6464

Web site: http://www.state.nj.us/state/
   museum

E-mail: feedback@sos.state.nj.us

Hadrosaurus

NEW MEXICO

RUTH HALL MUSEUM OF PALEONTOLOGY

In addition to a fossil collection that highlights the 225-million-year-old *Coelophysis* bone beds at Ghost Ranch, this museum, curated by famed paleontologist J. Lynett Gillette, also has a wonderful collection of dinosaur art, featuring the work of Margaret Colbert, Doug Henderson, Dave Thomas, and Greg Paul, and a photo archive with 4,000 pictures.

> Ghost Ranch Conference Center, U.S. 84
> HC 77, Box 11
> Abiquiu, NM 87510
> (505) 685-4333
> Web site: http://www.nmculture.org/cgi-bin/instview.cgi
>   ?_recordnum=RUTH
> E-mail: NA

NEW MEXICO MUSEUM OF NATURAL HISTORY AND SCIENCE

Discover the magic of prehistory at this top-notch New Mexico museum. The museum's many dinosaur exhibits focus on Jurassic dinosaurs, including *Seismosaurus, Brachiosaurus, Allosaurus, Stegosaurus,* and the Triassic *Coelophysis* (New Mexico's official state fossil). A Cretaceous display looks at a seaside New Mexico teeming with marine animals, strange birds, early mammals, and dinosaurs—including a jawbone with teeth from a *T. rex*. Other exhibits explore the effects of volcanoes and the Ice Age in New Mexico. The Ice Age exhibit illustrates how strange animals like dire wolves, mammoths, saber-toothed cats, and New Mexico's last camel thrived—then vanished.

1801 Mountain Rd. NW
Albuquerque, NM 87104
(505) 841-2800
Web site: http://www.museums.state.nm.us/nmmnh
E-mail: tim.aydelott@.state.nm.us

THE UNIVERSITY OF NEW MEXICO GEOLOGY MUSEUM

Dinosaur tracks and *Coelophysis* skeletal casts are the key points of this small museum's paleontology collection. But its sister museum, the Meteorite Museum, is well worth exploring, with a display of dozens of amazing meteorites that have struck the Earth. Considering that meteoric activity helped drive the dinosaurs into extinction, it seems fitting that it be included in this book.

Northrop Hall, Rm. 124
Albuquerque, NM 87131
(505) 277-4204
Web site: http://epswww.unm.edu/museum.htm
E-mail: epsdept@unm.edu

BONE DIGGER BONUS

DINOSAUR STOMPEDE

Looking for a great way to raise money for your favorite dinosaur museum? Follow New Mexico's lead. The 2003 Dinosaur Stompede was, according to the New Mexico Museum of Natural History and Science, a thunderous success.

What was the Dinosaur Stompede? Well, first a gathering of local artists customized more than one hundred 5-foot-tall fiberglass dinosaur models, based on either the Seismosaurus *or the* Pentaceratops *models in front of the museum (designed by local artist Dennis Liberty).*

Once complete, the dinos were put on display during the Dinosaur Stompede festival of events. The fancy fellas then "migrated" to locations in and around Albuquerque to inspire dinosaur devotion. Proceeds raised through ticket sales, entry fees, donations, and the sale of the dinosaur models went to the New Mexico Museum of Natural History and Science. But the fun should last for years and years.

Coelophysis

CLAYTON LAKE STATE PARK

According to the park's Web site, "Along the spillway, more than 500 dinosaur footprints have been preserved and identified. Plant-eating and carnivorous dinosaurs, as well as some ancient crocodiles, made these prints. Interpretive markers identify significant tracks and paleontological features on the walk. The best times to view the tracks are in the morning and late afternoon."

> 141 Clayton Lake Rd.
> Clayton, NM 88415
> (505) 374-8808
> Web site: http://www.emnrd.state.nm.us/nmparks/pages/parks/
> clayton/Clayton.htm
> E-mail: cjordan@state.nm.us

E³ CHILDREN'S MUSEUM (A PART OF THE FARMINGTON MUSEUM SYSTEM)

This hands-on children's museum is right in the heart of dinosaur country. Is it any wonder it has a yearly kids' camp for budding young paleontologists? Make that very young—three to six years old! Kids handle real fossils and hunt for fantasy dinosaur eggs. There is even a summer dinosaur reading program.

> 302 N. Orchard Ave.
> Farmington, NM 87401
> (505) 599-1425
> Web site: http://www.farmingtonmuseum.org/childrens.html
> E-mail: crwilliams@fmtn.org (Crystal Williams, museum
> coordinator)

FARMINGTON MUSEUM

Don't miss the Farmington Museum's Dinosaurs to Drillbits: The Oil and Gas Experience of San Juan Basin exhibit. It's a great way to understand how two natural resources are connected.

> 3041 E. Main St.
> Farmington, NM 87402
> (505) 599-1174
> Web site: http://www.farmingtonmuseum.org
> E-mail: dmeyers@fmtn.org
> (Dave Meyers, education coordinator)

Glyptodon

FOLSOM MUSEUM

When "Folsom Man"—the first real evidence of an Ice Age, nomadic tribe of people—was discovered at Dead Horse Gulch, it caused a paleo-stir in New Mexico. This museum—conceptualized in 1965—is dedicated to that discovery, and to other regional history. No dinosaurs, but of prehistoric importance just the same. Visitors are by appointment only.

PO Box 385

Folsom, NM 88419

(505) 278-2122

Web site: http://www.folsommuseum.netfirms.com

E-mail: vrb317@bacavalley.com

BLACKWATER DRAW MUSEUM

The Blackwater Draw archaeological site is considered one of the most important in the New World, highlighting 13,000 years of prehistoric tribal behavior, including the hunting of mammoths. Other animals featured in exhibits include armadillos, beavers, camels, deer, dire wolves, four-pronged antelopes, ground sloths, llamas, peccaries, saber-toothed cats, short-faced bears, shovel-toothed amebelodons, and tapirs.

42987 Hwy. 70

Portales, NM 88130

(505) 562-2202

Web site: http://www.enmu.edu/academics/excellence/
    museums/blackwater-draw

E-mail: webmaster@enmu.edu

MINERAL MUSEUM

There is a modest fossil display at this mineral museum, but the vast majority of exhibit space is dedicated to the amazing geologic resources of New Mexico, including the gold, silver, and precious gems the invading Spanish conquistadors were in search of. Specimens from the School of Mines dating back to 1889 are included in the museum's collection.

New Mexico Bureau of Geology and Mineral Resources

200W—Workman Addition

New Mexico Tech Campus

Socorro, NM 87801

(505) 835-5420

Web site: http://www.geoinfo.nmt.edu/education/museum

E-mail: vwlueth@nmt.edu (Dr. Virgil W. Lueth, curator)

MESALANDS DINOSAUR MUSEUM

Torvosaurus, Acrocanthosaurus, Triceratops, and *Tyrannosaurus rex* are just a few of the dinosaurs exhibited in this small museum, formed by a cooperative effort between the Mesalands Community College and citizens devoted to creating an educational outreach in the area. But what makes this museum really unique is the largest collection of (touchable) bronze dinosaur sculptures in the country. The college art department creates them on campus as part of the cooperative effort.

Mesalands Community College

222 E. Laughlin St.

Tucumcari, NM 88401

(505) 461-3466

Web site: http://www.mesalands.edu/museum/museum.htm

E-mail: NA

> **THE NEW MEXICO BUREAU OF GEOLOGY AND MINERAL RESOURCES**
> 2808 CENTRAL AVE. SE
> ALBUQUERQUE, NM 87106
> (505) 366-2530
> WEB SITE: HTTP://GEOINFO.NMT.EDU
> E-MAIL: ADAMREAD@GIS.NMT.EDU

NEW YORK

NEW YORK STATE MUSEUM

There's something a "little" amazing about the exhibit Ancient Life of New York—A Billion Years of Earth History. That's because this creative look at ancient history explores even fossil bacteria—some of the tiniest forms of prehistoric marine life that thrived 100 million years ago. Add ancient tree stumps, spiders, trilobites, and a full range of more traditional dinosaur and prehistoric mammal specimens, and you have a truly big new perspective on New York State.

Cultural Education Center

Rm. 3023

Empire State Plaza

Albany, NY 12230

(518) 474-5877

Web site: http://www.nysm.nysed.gov

E-mail: agnidica@mail.nysed.gov

BUFFALO MUSEUM OF SCIENCE

The Buffalo Museum of Science's Dinosaurs and Co. exhibit is divided into four sections on prehistoric exploration: the Early Seas; Conquest of the Land; the Age of Dinosaurs; and the Age of Mammals, reflecting nearly every phase of prehistory. You'll encounter "Lucy"—one of the earliest human ancestors ever unearthed—and rare fossilized plants and sea animals, as well as *Tyrannosaurus rex, Triceratops, Allosaurus,* and other dinosaurs.

1020 Humboldt Pkwy.

Buffalo, NY 14211

(716) 896-5200

Web site: http://www.sciencebuff.org

E-mail: kleacock@sciencebuff.org

PALEONTOLOGICAL RESEARCH INSTITUTION

In 2003, the PRI debuted its remarkable Museum of the Earth, mapping out 4.5 billion years of natural history for all the world to see. Besides fossils and dinosaur mounts drawn from the extensive prehistoric collection overseen by the PRI, there is an amazing 560-panel mural painted by acclaimed artist Barbara Page. Each panel represents 1 million years of history on Earth. A working fossil-preparation lab makes it possible for visitors to understand the art of separating rock from ancient bone and plant matter. Take a virtual tour of the new museum on the PRI's Web site. But be sure to visit the real thing when you're in Ithaca.

Museum of the Earth

1259 Trumansburg Rd.

Ithaca, NY 14850

(607) 273-6623

Web site: http://www.priweb.org

E-mail: webmaster@museumoftheearth.org

AMERICAN MUSEUM OF NATURAL HISTORY

According to museum literature, the museum's newly renovated Fossil Halls "display the single largest and most diverse array of vertebrate fossils in the world." Stroll back 500 million years as you examine the vertebrate "family tree." From the towering 145-million-year-old *Barosaurus* defending her baby from a meat-eating *Allosaurus* to the loyal oviraptorid that died while guarding her eggs (found by the museum in 1994 in Mongolia's Gobi Desert), each mounted skeleton and display is amazing and unforgettable—a must-see.

Oviraptorid

> Central Park West at Seventy-ninth St.
> New York, NY 10024
> (212) 769-5100
> Web site: http://www.amnh.org
> E-mail: form on Web site

NEW YORK PALEONTOLOGICAL SOCIETY

For more information about New York State's fossil resources, contact or join the New York Paleontological Society.

> Planetarium Station
> PO Box 287
> 127 W. Eighty-third St.
> New York, NY 10024
> Web site: http://www.nyps.org
> E-mail: info@nyps.org

NATURAL STONE BRIDGE AND CAVES

Strolling into caves that have been carved through Earth's geology for millions of years is always a little awe-inspiring. Strolling through these New York wonders is especially engaging because the geological formations are so diverse. The facility's trout brook bubbles through and under the Ponte de Dios (Bridge of God) rock formations, only to resurface 500 feet downstream into Artist's Gorge, then Echo Cave, Garnet Cave, and the Cave of the Lost Pool. As the tour concludes in Noisy Cave, the brook has been transformed into a roaring waterway that vanishes beneath your feet. Fossils aren't really a part of the cave experience, but they are at the on-site Rock Shop and Fossil

Center. You can see a fossilized piranha fish, a saber-toothed cat skull, and a giant cave bear paw. Dinosaur bone samples and petrified wood are for sale, along with crystals, geodes, and geology books.

Stone Bridge Rd.
Pottersville, NY 12860
(518) 494-2283
Web site: http://www.stonebridgeandcaves.com
E-mail: NA

BONE DIGGER BONUS

DINOSAUR DREAMS COME TRUE

by Dr. Bryn J. Mader
Assistant Professor, Queensboro Community College

As long as I can remember, I have loved extinct animals, especially dinosaurs. My parents brought me to the American Museum [of Natural History] often as a child. In fact, I often begged them to take me. They always encouraged my interest. From high school on, I knew I wanted to be a professional paleontologist and I spent my college and graduate years training for this career.

In recent years, I have been privileged to work in the museum that I loved so much as a child—the American Museum of Natural History. I spent my days caring for the massive collections of fossils kept mostly behind the scenes, and thus rarely seen by the public.

Initially, I worked for the Department of Vertebrate Paleontology. Then I worked as collections registrar for the Department of Vertebrate Mammalogy. It was an honor to care for these collections and a great responsibility. The collections of the American Museum [of Natural History] have taken well over a century to build, and they are irreplaceable. It was my job to ensure that they are preserved for posterity, so that future generations will always have them to learn from and enjoy.

My research includes the dinosaurs and titanotheres—an extinct relative of the horse and rhino with large, forked horns. Paleontology is a fascinating subject and I can't think of a more rewarding career for a young person to enter.

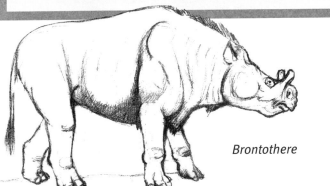

Brontothere

NORTH CAROLINA

AURORA FOSSIL MUSEUM

One of the few dino-destinations to give you something prehistoric to *take home,* the Aurora Fossil Museum lets you look for your own fossilized shark teeth from materials hauled in from local phosphate mines. Beyond these amazing keepsakes, you'll see exhibits and audiovisual presentations about ancient marine life.

> 400 Main St.
> Aurora, NC 27806
> (252) 322-4238
> Web site: http://www.pamlico.com/
>   aurora/fossils
> E-mail: NA

DISCOVERY PLACE

Robotic dinosaurs, including *Apatosaurus, Pachycephalosaurus, Stegosaurus, Triceratops,* and *Tyrannosaurus rex,* and prehistoric reptile *Dimetrodon,* are a permanent part of the Discovery Place's hands-on exhibits.

Pachycephalosaurus

Powered by compressed air, they represent a kind of dinosaur model that's fading from view. So check them out before they go extinct. Great fun and reasonably good science.

> 301 N. Tryon St.
> Charlotte, NC 28202
> (704) 372-6261
> Web site: http://www.discoveryplace.org
> E-mail: info@discoveryplace.org

MUSEUM OF LIFE AND SCIENCE

The museum's geology exhibit promises the chance to investigate the properties of rocks, gems, minerals, and dinosaur fossils. And a small group of classic "Americana" outdoor dinosaur models offers great photo opportunities for the whole family (even if the models were sculpted before modern dinosaur theory came into play). As a side note, don't miss the Magic Wings Butterfly House—a must-see while you're there digging dinosaurs.

> 433 Murray Ave.
> Durham, NC 27704
> (919) 220-5429
> Web site: http://www.ncmls.org
> E-mail: contactus@ncmls.org

RANKIN MUSEUM OF AMERICAN AND NATURAL HISTORY

A great cross section of prehistoric fossils, including a giant crocodile skull from the Cretaceous, crinoids, a *Mosasaurus* (a marine reptile), lungfish, trilobites, and ammonites, are on display in this growing museum's paleontology collection. It's a delightful small museum worth visiting if you're nearby.

> 131 W. Church St.
> Ellerbe, NC 28338
> (910) 652-6378
> Web site: http://www.rankinmuseum.com
> E-mail: info@rankinmuseum.com

SCHIELE MUSEUM OF NATURAL HISTORY AND PLANETARIUM

The museum's Hall of Earth and Man—created in 1988—offers a great overview of 500 million years of history on Earth through models, graphics, fossils, artifacts, and interpretive texts. Especially interesting is the early-mammal display and old-school *Tyrannosaurus rex* model, complete with drooping tail.

1500 E. Garrison Blvd.

Gastonia, NC 28054

(704) 866-6900

Web site: http://www.schielemuseum.org

E-mail: info@schielemuseum.org

NORTH CAROLINA MUSEUM OF NATURAL SCIENCES

From the ferocity of *Acrocanthosaurus* to the tender heart of "Willo"—the small, plant-eating *Thescelosaurus* found with what may be a fossilized heart—this museum, first opened in April 2000, is a dinosaur lover's dream, thanks in part to dinosaur expert Dr. Dale Russell. It's not all dinosaurs, by any stretch. But what's there is new and vibrant and full of amazing detail.

11 W. Jones St.

Raleigh, NC 27601

(919) 733-7450

Web site: http://www.naturalsciences.org

Alternate Web site: http://www.dinoheart.org (Willo site)

E-mail: museum@naturalsciences.org

SCIWORKS

Exploring fossils and minerals is possible through this hands-on museum's Science Lab exhibit, which includes a simulated fossil dig. You can also explore the physics of erosion (a process that makes finding fossils possible) through its sand dune demonstration.

400 W. Hanes Mill Rd.

Winston-Salem, NC 27105

(336) 767-6730

Web site: http://www.sciworks.org

E-mail: info@sciworks.org

Acrocanthosaurus

BONE DIGGER BONUS

A DAY IN THE LIFE OF WILLO

by Dr. Dale Russell
Senior Curator of Paleontology, NC Museum of Natural Sciences

Author's Note: Dr. Dale Russell has been entrusted with "Willo," a 66-million-year-old Thescelosaurus *found in South Dakota with what may be her heart fossilized along with her bones. We asked Dr. Russell what an average day in a dinosaur like Willo's life might have been like. This is how he responded. For more on Willo, visit http://www.dinoheart.org.*

The little animal was a herbivore that carefully selected (and chopped up) the vegetation that it browsed. It was very well adapted (streamlined body, short powerful legs) for rapid escape into underbrush. Its brain was relatively small, so you could expect its behavior to be similar to that one could image as typical for a giant turtle. On the islands of the southwestern Pacific, turtles would probably be buried in shallow pits and roasted with yams until tender. So Willo was probably sought by Cretaceous carnivores as well. I once found the skeleton of a baby dinosaur that resembled Willo, so I imagine they nested in warm wetlands like those along the Carolina-Georgia coast.

Thescelosaurus

NORTH CAROLINA GEOLOGICAL SURVEY
DIVISION OF LAND RESOURCES
1612 MAIL SERVICE CENTER
RALEIGH, NC 27699
(919) 733-2423
WEB SITE: HTTP://WWW.GEOLOGY.ENR.STATE.NC.US
E-MAIL: NA

NORTH DAKOTA

STATE HISTORICAL SOCIETY OF NORTH DAKOTA

Thanks to the North Dakota Geological Survey, this lovely local museum has several exceptional fossil displays, along with exhibits of state history. A partial *Triceratops* skull, a mastodon, and a remarkable mosasaur are all mounted and beautifully exhibited in the museum's Corridor of Time exhibit.

> 612 E. Boulevard Ave.
> Bismarck, ND 58505
> (701) 328-2666
> Web site: http://www.state.nd.us/hist
> E-mail: histsoc@state.nd.us

PIONEER TRAILS REGIONAL MUSEUM

Not only are fossils (including dinosaurs, mosasaurs, and other prehistoric animals) on exhibit at this small-town history museum, but a summer field school offers visitors the chance to dig for dinosaurs and other prehistoric fossils alongside trained, expert staffers, for a fee, in July and August. Kids under eighteen must be accompanied by an adult, but it's a terrific opportunity to learn about paleontology firsthand. There are also day tours of the dig site for fossil fans with a little less time to invest—a great and rare opportunity.

> 12 First Ave. NE
> Bowman, ND 58623
> (701) 523-3600
> Web site: http://www.ptrm.org
> E-mail: ptrm@ptrm.org

DAKOTA DINOSAUR MUSEUM

Devoted expressly to dinosaurs, this 13,400-square-foot museum is pure dino-heaven. New Mexico artist Dave Thomas's sculpted *Triceratops* guards the door. Full skeletal casts of *Allosaurus, Albertosaurus, Thescelosaurus,* and *Stegosaurus* were made by Salt Lake City's Dino Lab. Texas artist John Fischner fleshed out sculptures of *Coelophysis, Deinonychus, Dromaeosaurus, Velociraptor, Archaeopteryx,* and *Compsognathus.* And North Dakota artists Jack Stewart and Lili Stewart-Wheeler painted a beautiful *Tyrannosaurus rex* and *Triceratops* mural and a bison and rhinoceros mural. Thousands of actual fossil specimens round out the museum and make it a perfect blend of art and science.

200 Museum Dr.
Dickinson, ND 58601
(701) 225-3466
Web site: http://www.dakotadino.com
E-mail: info@dakotadino.com

Deinonychus

THEODORE ROOSEVELT NATIONAL PARK

According to the National Park Service Web site, "The fossilized remains of a 4-foot reptile known as *Champsosaurus* were excavated from a hillside in the South Unit in October 1995 by Dr. John Hoganson, state paleontologist, and his assistant, Jonathan Campbell. The ancient crocodile-like reptile once

BONE DIGGER BONUS

MOSASAUR FAST FACTS

(Courtesy of the North Dakota Heritage Center)

- *Mosasaurs were huge—some as long as 40 feet—and inhabited the world's oceans during the Cretaceous Period, from about 90 million to 65 million years ago. They were a large group of reptiles that included many species.*
- *Nicknamed the "Tyrannosaurus rex of the Sea," they probably preyed on other mosasaurs, fish, turtles, and invertebrates.*
- *Although not dinosaurs, these lizard-like reptiles lived at the same time and became extinct when the dinosaurs did. They thrived for about 25 million years.*
- *The 23-foot-long mosasaur on permanent exhibit at the North Dakota Heritage Center in Bismarck was discovered in 1995 near Cooperstown, North Dakota.*
- *The fossil at the North Dakota Heritage Center is of the genus, or group, of mosasaurs known as* Plioplatecarpus, *and is a new species of this genus that has not been found anywhere else in the world. It is also 25 percent larger than any other known mosasaur in this* Plioplatecarpus *group.*
- *After it died, its carcass was scavenged by dogfish (a kind of shark), as indicated by the tens of thousands of dogfish teeth found with the mosasaur skeleton and gnaw marks on some of its bones.*
- *Other creatures that lived in the oceans that covered North Dakota during the time of the mosasaurs included sharks, rays, plesiosaurs, turtles, sea birds, and invertebrates such as snails, lobsters, coral, and clams.*
- *Mosasaurs are believed to be closely related to the largest known lizards alive today, the Komodo dragons of Indonesia, which measure up to 10 feet long.*

inhabited the freshwaters in what is now western North Dakota about 55 million years ago during the Paleocene Epoch. This was a time when the climate was subtropical, similar to that of present-day Florida." You can see the beautiful mounted skeleton of that prehistoric reptile at the Theodore Roosevelt National Park visitors center, along with other fossils common to the region.

PO Box 7
Medora, ND 58645
(701) 623-4466 (South Unit info.)
(701) 842-2333 (North Unit info.)
Web site: http://www.nps.gov/thro
E-mail: form on Web site

NORTH DAKOTA GEOLOGICAL SURVEY
600 E. BOULEVARD AVE.
BISMARCK, ND 58505
(701) 328-8000
WEB SITE: HTTP://WWW.STATE.ND.US/NDGS
FOSSIL WEB SITE: HTTP://WWW.STATE.ND.US/NDFOSSILS
E-MAIL: NDGSWEBMASTER@STATE.ND.US

OHIO

WM. McKINLEY PRESIDENTIAL LIBRARY AND MUSEUM

Though this museum is dedicated primarily to the state history of Ohio and U.S. President William McKinley, its Discovery World includes some good dinosaur resources, including an *Allosaurus* model, a play cave (on Natural History Island) modeled after a *Tyrannosaurus rex* skull, and mastodon remains in the Paleo-Indian arena.

800 McKinley Monument Dr. NW
Canton, OH 44708

(330) 455-7043
Web site: http://www.mckinleymuseum.org
E-mail: form on Web site

CINCINNATI MUSEUM CENTER

Ever wanted to walk through an Ice Age? Visit this museum and you'll get your wish—*almost.* Cincinnati's Ice Age: Clues Frozen in Time is a wonderful exhibit that reviews 19,000 years of prehistory, when the Ohio Valley was in the throes of a glacial retreat, with sheets of ice sliding across the landscape. A working fossil lab helps explain the process of preparing those clues for study. And the Lost Voices exhibit helps interpret what fossils tell us once they're unearthed and studied.

Museum of Natural History and Science

1301 Western Ave.

Cincinnati, OH 45203

(800) 733-2077

(513) 287-7000

Web site: http://www.cincymuseum.org

E-mail: exhibits@cincymuseum.org

THE CLEVELAND MUSEUM OF NATURAL HISTORY

Cleveland may be known for rock and roll, but Elvis isn't the only "King" in town. *Tyrannosaurus rex* reigns supreme at the Cleveland Museum of Natural History. (Actually, make that *Nanotyrannus,* who is something like the prehistoric "crown prince.") A 70-foot-long *Haplocanthosaurus* backs up the meat-eater. And *Dunkleosteus,* a massive armored fish, also makes a splash.

1 Wade Oval Dr., University Circle

Cleveland, OH 44106

(216) 231-4600

Web site: http://www.cmnh.org

E-mail: info@cmnh.org

OHIO HISTORICAL CENTER

The Nature of Ohio exhibit reveals Ohio's natural history through plants, animals, geology, and geography. Included is the Conway mastodon, along with other fossil specimens common to prehistoric Ohio during the Ice Age and under an ancient sea.

Nanotyrannus

1982 Velma Ave.

Columbus, OH 43211

(614) 297-2300

Web site: http://www.ohiohistory.org/places/ohc

E-mail: form on Web site

BOONSHOFT MUSEUM OF DISCOVERY

Dayton is world famous for some of the most amazing trilobites ever unearthed, and the Boonshoft Museum of Discovery has many of them on display. It also offers a mastodon dig simulation, complete with a "field station" in the second-floor exhibit space. While you're there, don't miss the Ohio Division of Wildlife's peregrine falcon exhibit, dedicated to helping celebrate and protect Mercury, a thirteen-year-old beauty, and his mate, Snowball.

2600 DeWeese Pkwy.

Dayton, OH 45414

(937) 275-7431

Web site: http://www.boonshoftmuseum.org

E-mail: NA

BONE DIGGER BONUS

SOMETHING "BUGGING" ANCIENT OHIO

Ohio's state fossil may be a trilobite, but in the late 1990s, Ohio State University paleontologists came across something amazing from a coal mine on the eastern side of the state. Preserved along with hundreds of other Carboniferous fossils was a giant, 300-million-year-old cockroach—the largest known fossil cockroach.

"Normally, we can only hope to find fossils of shell and bone, because they have minerals in them that increase their chances for preservation," said Ohio State student Cary Easterday in a 2001 university press release. "But something unusual about the chemistry of this ancient site preserved organisms without shell or bones with incredible detail."

Veins in the insect's wings, bumps covering the wing surfaces, antennae, and even a tiny mouth are visible in the one-of-a-kind cockroach fossil found at a dig site at the intersection of Ohio State Routes 7 and 11.

How big is this giant? It measures out at 3.5 inches long. Considering today's average North American cockroach tops out at about 1 inch, the coal mine cockroach was a whopper—a big bug that lived long, long before the dinosaur giants.

The largest cockroaches of all time (that we know about) live today in Central and South America. The longest ones are almost 4 inches!

FOSSIL PRESERVE PARK

Finding (and keeping) Devonian trilobites, brachiopods, and coral specimens 375 million years old is easy, thanks to the development of Sylvania's Fossil Preserve Park, managed by the Olander Park system. Visitors to these shale beds (not far from Toledo) can search for and keep fossils they find. The town of Sylvania also hosts a yearly "Fossil Fest" in September to celebrate the park and other paleo-activities.

> (on Centennial Rd. near Sylvania-Metamora Rd.)
>
> Sylvania, OH 43560
>
> (419) 882-8313
>
> Web site: http://www.olanderpk.com and
>   http://www.cityofsylvania.com/Parks/cparklst.htm
>
> E-mail: city.parks@sev.org

CAESAR CREEK LAKE SPILLWAY

Another rare opportunity to collect prehistoric fossils you can keep presents itself at Ohio's Caesar Creek Lake Spillway, located within Caesar Creek State Park. Natural erosion reveals the secrets of an ancient sea, swimming with brachiopods, cephalopods, bryozoans, gastropods, crinoids, horn coral, and trilobites. Tiny samples of each fossil can be collected. But there are a few rules: You must obtain a free permit at the visitors center. No tools can be used for collection. Fossils cannot be collected for commercial purposes. You can keep only as much as will fit in the palm of your hand. Collecting outside the spillway is not allowed. And climbing the spillway walls is prohibited (and dangerous!).

> 8570 E. S.R. 73
>
> Waynesville, OH 45068
>
> (513) 897-3055
>
> Web site: http://www.dnr.state.ohio.us/parks/parks/caesarck.htm
>
> E-mail: NA

OHIO GEOLOGICAL SURVEY
OHIO DEPARTMENT OF NATURAL RESOURCES
2045 MORSE RD., BLDG. C
COLUMBUS, OH 43229
(614) 265-6576
WEB SITE: HTTP://WWW.DNR.STATE.OH.US/GEOSURVEY
E-MAIL: GEO.SURVEY@DNR.STATE.OH.US

CIMARRON HERITAGE CENTER

Though this is a historical museum dedicated to the rich history of the Texas/Oklahoma panhandle region, part of that proud heritage includes dinosaur trackways left by long-necked sauropods. To celebrate that aspect of the Boise City story, check out "Cimmy"—a huge, stylized steel sculpture of a "Brontosaurus" standing watch outside the center, funded by local writer Norma Jean Young.

> PO Box 214
> 1300 N. Cimarron (Hwy. 287 N.)
> Boise City, OK 73933
> (580) 544-3479
> Web site: http://www.ptsi.net/user/museum/chc.html
> E-mail: NA

BLACK MESA STATE PARK

Named for a thick layer of black lava, this 1,600-acre wildlife preserve represents 140 million years of geologic history. Scattered with dinosaur footprints and other fossil resources, the park has hosted numerous productive paleo-digs, including a "Brontosaurus" (*Apatosaurus*) skeleton. A replica of a 6-foot-long femur, or leg bone, that weighed more than 400 pounds is on display on State Highway 325, about 8 miles east of Kenton.

> County Rd. 325
> Kenton, OK 73946
> (800) 654-8240
> (580) 426-2222
> Web site: http://www.touroklahoma.com/parks.asp
> E-mail: rsrtpark@otrd.state.ok.us or blackmesa@ptsi.net

THE SAM NOBLE OKLAHOMA MUSEUM OF NATURAL HISTORY

Dinosaurs once thundered across the landscape that became modern Oklahoma. They left behind enough fossil evidence—skeletal remains and tracks—to help inspire the museum's Hall of Ancient Life exhibit, a walk through prehistoric time. Featured dinosaurs include *Apatosaurus* and *Pentaceratops* and others in dramatic skeletal poses. The Pleistocene Plaza moves us forward to study early man and his interaction with the Columbian mammoth.

> 2401 Chautauqua Ave.
> Norman, OK 73072

(405) 325-4712
Web site: http://www.snomnh.ou.edu
E-mail: snomnh@ou.edu

BONE DIGGER BONUS

OKIE TRACKS TO EXPLORE

by Norma Jean Young
Town Historian and Author, Boise City

I was six years old when dinosaur fossils were uncovered 8 miles east of Kenton (30 miles northwest of Boise City) in 1931. The best find was a skeleton of a 70-foot-long Apatosaurus.

Dinosaur tracks were also found embedded in rock in a streambed northeast of Kenton. This was even better, as far as the kids were concerned, because this was something that would stay here. *We could see them anytime we wanted to.*

We now have bus tours to the Kenton area early in June, and the tourists and locals never tire of slipping and sliding down the arroyos to view the huge tracks. They realize, "I am walking where a dinosaur once walked."

Some experts believed the dinosaur finds here were farther east than any other North American discoveries from the Late Jurassic Period, and that if it were possible to use a giant scraper to take off the top layer of soil over most of Cimarron County, thousands more dinosaur fossils would be exposed.

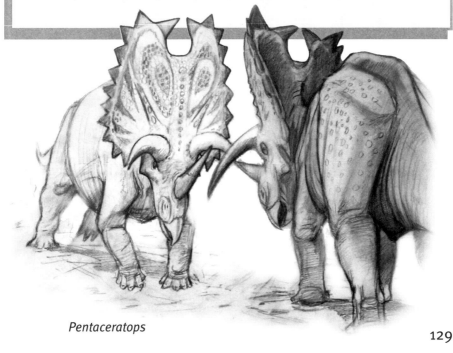

Pentaceratops

129

OKLAHOMA GEOLOGICAL SURVEY
100 E. BOYD ST.
STE. N131
NORMAN, OK 73019
(800) 330-3996
(405) 325-3031
WEB SITE: HTTP://WWW.OGS.OU.EDU
E-MAIL: OGS-WEB@GCN.OU.EDU

 **OREGON**

THE HIGH DESERT MUSEUM

Oregon's fossil history is part of this museum's calling, but one of the most distinctive offerings is the Fossil Detective family workshop, where participants are encouraged to study the prehistoric animals of Oregon through fossil searches, then create a small fossil collection to keep.

> 59800 S. Hwy. 97
> Bend, OR 97702
> (541) 382-4754
> Web site: http://www.highdesertmuseum.org
> E-mail: form on Web site

CRATER ROCK MUSEUM

Founded in 1954 by Frieda and Delmar Smith, this small museum is packed full of fascinating mineral information. Fossil eggs, bones, teeth, and dung, some dating back 500 million years, are on display. Petrified wood and other fossils are also part of the collection. The gift shop offers visitors the chance to buy fossils of their own.

> 2002 Scenic Ave.
> Central Point, OR 97502
> (541) 664-6081
> Web site: http://www.craterrock.com
> E-mail: NA

CONDON MUSEUM

The Reverend Thomas Condon, an amateur fossil collector, helped U.S. cavalry troops identify fossils from the John Day Valley in the summer of 1861. Intrigued by what he saw, it wasn't long before he, too, headed for the fossil beds. Soon he was corresponding with Bone War giants Edward Drinker Cope, O. C. Marsh, and Joseph Leidy as well. This fossil collection, named for Condon, reveals the rich prehistory of Oregon—a history too often overlooked.

> Department of Geological Sciences
> Cascade Hall
> University of Oregon
> Eugene, OR 97403
> (541) 346-4577
> Web site: http://www.uoregon.edu/~dogsci/
>   facilities/condon.html
> E-mail: NA

MUSEUM OF NATURAL HISTORY

According to the museum's Web site, "Rock hounds young and old can explore Oregon's turbulent geology and view fossils and rocks that glow in the dark." In February 2004, the University of Oregon Museum of Natural History completely redesigned its main exhibit hall. As you walk through the updated displays, you are connected to the geologic past of the region, including explorations of Oregon's ancient animals and tribal ancestors.

> University of Oregon
> 1680 E. Fifteenth Ave.
> Eugene, OR 97403
> (541) 346-3024
> Web site: http://natural-history.uoregon.edu
> E-mail: mnh@uoregon.edu

RICE NORTHWEST MUSEUM OF ROCKS AND MINERALS

Petrified wood, fossil palms, and cycad specimens—polished and beautifully displayed—are a part of this museum's fossil resources.

> 26385 NW Groveland Dr.
> Hillsboro, OR 97124
> (503) 647-2418
> Web site: http://www.ricenwmuseum.org
> E-mail: info@ricenwmuseum.org

VOLCANIC DISASTER

by Ted Fremd
Paleontologist, John Day Fossil Beds National Monument

The John Day Fossil Beds National Monument consists of three different geographically sep-arate areas, or units: Sheep Rock, Painted Hills, and Clarno. Among the three of them, over 40 million years are chronicled.

With climates shifting from para-tropical to a cool, high desert, the diversity of the plant and animal fossils represented in this fossil record is very large. There are several trails, a visitors center, and research facilities at the monument.

The opportunity to perceive and work with the ecosystems against a backdrop of such "deep time" is tremendously rewarding. Discovering, uncovering, and curating new speci-mens into public repositories is always of interest. But it is the analysis of the biota—plants and animals of the region—on a grander scale that is most inspiring.

JOHN DAY FOSSIL BEDS NATIONAL MONUMENT

Oregon may not be rich in dinosaur fossils, but it has experienced its fair share of volcanic destruction. And even a quick look at the John Day Fossil Beds National Monument proves it. About 40 to 65 million years ago, during the Cenozoic Era, alligators, three-toed horses, pigs, dogs, cats, camels, rodents, and other prehistoric animals thrived in what became Kimberly, Oregon. Then disaster struck. As volcanic ash buried an enormous cross sec-tion of ancient life, what would become the John Day Fossil Beds National Monument was born. A visitors center helps illustrate the value of this fossil stop, even without a single dinosaur in the mix.

> 32651 Hwy. 19
> Kimberly, OR 97848
> (541) 987-2333
> Web site: http://www.nps.gov/joda
> E-mail: form on Web site

THE GEOLOGICAL SOCIETY OF THE OREGON COUNTRY

Dinosaurs are not normally a part of Oregon's geological history. But there are *other* fossil experiences to be had in the Pacific Northwest, and this Portland-based organization takes advantage through lectures and field trips. See its Web site for more information.

PO Box 907
Portland, OR 97207
Web site: http://www.gsoc.org
E-mail: NA

OREGON MUSEUM OF SCIENCE AND INDUSTRY

This hands-on science museum offers Earth Science Hall, complete with fossil replicas, a Paleo Lab, and a staff of volunteers preparing real dinosaur and ancient Oregon fossils for scientific study in a setting visible to the museum public.

1945 SE Water Ave.
Portland, OR 97214
(800) 955-6674
(503) 797-6674
Web site: http://www.omsi.edu
E-mail: form on Web site

PREHISTORIC GARDENS

Nestled among the lush rain forest ferns of coastal Oregon are more than a dozen prehistoric concrete-over-wire-mesh sculptures based on fossil information from the 1950s. Vividly painted to reflect artist E. V. Nelson's own thinking, they stand out in the woods, as much a symbol of the changing field of dinosaur science as they are representative of the species themselves.

(Hwy. 101, between Port Orford and Gold Beach)
Port Orford, OR 97465
(541) 332-4463
Web site: NA
E-mail: NA

DOUGLAS COUNTY MUSEUM OF HISTORY
AND NATURAL HISTORY

A very limited number of prehistoric fossils are on display at this small-town history museum, including ancient fern fossils.

123 Museum Dr.
Roseburg, OR 97470
(541) 957-7007
Web site: http://www.co.douglas.or.us/museum
E-mail: museum@co.douglas.or.us

PENNSYLVANIA

THE NORTH MUSEUM OF NATURAL HISTORY AND SCIENCE

This vibrant local museum has a Dinosaur Hall of its very own, featuring fossils and a partial model of a *Tyrannosaurus rex*. It's a fun stop for families. Don't miss the live animal room, complete with reptiles, amphibians, and insects.

400 College Ave.

Lancaster, PA 17603

(717) 291-3941

Web site: http://www.northmuseum.org

E-mail: info@northmuseum.org

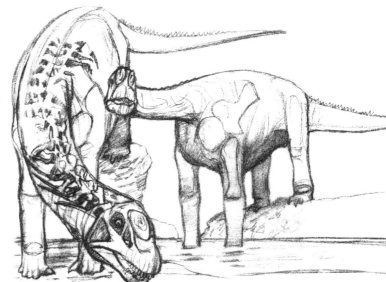

Camarasaurus

THE ACADEMY OF NATURAL SCIENCES

In March 1998, the Academy of Natural Sciences unveiled its updated Dinosaur Hall to the delight of millions. The presentation vividly details the Age of the Dinosaurs—160 million years of evolutionary success, and their seemingly sudden extinction. Six important new fossil skeletons were added, including *Giganotosaurus,* a recently discovered carnivore slightly larger than *T. rex.* Several hands-on exhibits about fossil collection and cataloging complement the displays to make this a first-rate dinosaur adventure.

1900 Benjamin Franklin Pkwy.

Philadelphia, PA 19103

(215) 299-1000

Web site: http://www.acnatsci.org

E-mail: webmaster@acnatsci.org

WAGNER FREE INSTITUTE OF SCIENCE

Dinosaur fossils are exhibited at the Wagner Free Institute of Science, but part of what makes this place unique is the historical value of the building itself. Founded in 1855, the museum has remained essentially unaltered for 150 years.

1700 W. Montgomery Ave.

Philadelphia, PA 19121

(215) 763-6529

Web site: http://www.wagnerfreeinstitute.org

E-mail: info@wagnerfreeinstitute.org

CARNEGIE MUSEUM OF NATURAL HISTORY

One of the world's best-known dinosaur collections is housed in the Carnegie Museum of Natural History's Dinosaur Hall. The visual feast begins with *Diplodocus* and *Apatosaurus,* two enormous long-necked plant-eaters. As if hungry for a meal itself, *Tyrannosaurus rex* stands nearby, in all its carnivorous glory. *Allosaurus,* a smaller bipedal meat-eater, is also there, as are *Stegosaurus, Dryosaurus, Camptosaurus,* and a juvenile *Camarasaurus*—the most complete sauropod skeleton ever found.

4400 Forbes Ave.

Pittsburgh, PA 15213

(412) 622-3131

Web site: http://www.clpgh.org/cmnh

E-mail: cmnhweb@carnegiemnh.org

BONE DIGGER BONUS

HOW TO BECOME A PALEONTOLOGIST

by Andrew D. Redline
Carnegie Museum of Natural History

Every year, many young, aspiring paleontologists write to me asking what are the proper steps to becoming a professional in the field. Answering these inquiries is one of my primary pleasures, and it illustrates what I believe the job is all about.

The best way to become a paleontologist is simple—decide you already are one. This may seem silly, but it helps open the door to the work that will follow. If you are really cut out to be a paleontologist, it won't seem like work. You will be surprised to learn what is possible when you're interested in the topic. Most paleontologists will admit that they have done much of their training on their own.

Being a paleontologist means being a detective of Earth history. All evidence bearing on the past must be considered. Anatomy and physiology are critical to understanding animal structure and relationships. Genetics and embryology help in unraveling the evolutionary process. Geology and chemistry help in understanding the material basis and environmental context of the Earth and its history of life. Even astronomy will help. The Earth is a product of the distribution of mass and energy in the universe, and what is possible on this planet is a function of these relationships. Don't just study or read about dinosaurs.

The last and most important point is to be interested in everything alive. The true paleontologist pictures extinct life at the time when it was living. Notice how insects, birds and flatworms live and relate to each other. How are they similar? How are they different? Why do very closely related coyotes and wolves live in different areas and have different social structures? How do clams have babies? Why does this work in the marine environment?

Nothing exists without its relationship to all that is around it and to what has come before. This includes those objects of popular worship—the dinosaurs. They were living animals, probably unique in comparison to the animals we know today. But, nevertheless, they were subject to the same rules and limitations. The knowledge of anything specific is impossible without the comparative bigger picture.

Earth history is a wonderful subject that will never be told in its entirety. The fun is in the wondering—not in the knowing. If that makes sense to you, then you will probably make a good paleontologist. Good luck!

THE FROST ENTOMOLOGICAL MUSEUM

While thousands and thousands of preserved insect specimens are on display at this amazing entomology museum, the prehistoric collection, representing the evolution of insects, will interest fossil fans most.

Department of Entomology
Pennsylvania State University
University Park, PA 16802
(814) 863-2865
Web site: http://www.ento.psu.edu/home/frost
E-mail: NA

PENNSYLVANIA GEOLOGICAL SURVEY
3240 SCHOOLHOUSE RD.
MIDDLETOWN, PA 17057
(717) 702-2017
WEB SITE: HTTP://WWW.DCNR.STATE.PA.US/TOPOGEO
E-MAIL: JAYPARRISH@STATE.PA.US
(JAY B. PARRISH, DIRECTOR AND STATE GEOLOGIST)

RHODE ISLAND

Contact the Rhode Island Geological Survey for information about field trips in and around the state to study prehistoric fossils.

RHODE ISLAND GEOLOGICAL SURVEY
9 E. ALUMNI AVE.
314 WOODWARD HALL
UNIVERSITY OF RHODE ISLAND
KINGSTON, RI 02881
(401) 874-2265
WEB SITE: HTTP://WWW.URI.EDU/CELS/GEO/RI_GEOLOGICAL_SURVEY.HTM
E-MAIL: RIGSURV@ETAL.URI.EDU

SOUTH CAROLINA

THE CHARLESTON MUSEUM

Lovingly called "America's First Museum," this South Carolina treasure celebrates the state's complete historical contribution, including dinosaurs and other fossil resources. Naturalists John James Audubon, André Michaux, Mark Catesby, and the Reverend John Bachman each spent time in the Charleston area or surrounds. Some of their collected specimens, including a primitive toothed whale, an 18-foot-long crocodile, and the second-largest known flying bird, are on display. These non-dinosaur fossils from 28-million-year-old marine beds near Charleston are proudly exhibited, along with a Cretaceous plant-eating dinosaur, *Thescelosaurus neglectus*.

> 360 Meeting St.
> Charleston, SC 29403
> (843) 722-2996
> Web site: http://www.charlestonmuseum.org
> E-mail: info@charlestonmuseum.org

BOB CAMPBELL GEOLOGY MUSEUM

Prehistoric displays featuring mammals, sharks and rays, plants, and shellfish are just a part of this university geology museum's exhibits. For example, did you know there were fossilized dolphin teeth? Prehistoric rabbits? There are . . . and they are part of this museum's extensive collection. This is a great little-known geological museum you shouldn't miss when you're in South Carolina.

> Clemson University
> 103 Garden Trail
> Clemson, SC 29634
> (864) 656-4600
> Web site: http://www.virtual.clemson.edu/groups/geomuseum
> E-mail: dcheech@clemson.edu (David Cicimurri, curator)

SOUTH CAROLINA STATE MUSEUM

For more than a decade, this state museum's natural history department has been collecting fossil specimens—including the first dinosaur fossils found in South Carolina—and a number of other dinosaur fossils for its Life in the Past exhibit. Also on display are Ice Age fossils, including a life-size mastodon. And don't miss the Great White Shark exhibit. It's amazing.

> 301 Gervais St.
> Columbia, SC 29214

(803) 898-4921
Web site: http://www.museum.state.sc.us
E-mail: publicrelations@museum.state.sc.us

U.S. GEOLOGICAL SURVEY, WRD
STEPHENSON CENTER, STE. 129
720 GRACERN RD.
COLUMBIA, SC 29210
(803) 750-6100
WEB SITE: HTTP://SC.WATER.USGS.GOV
E-MAIL: SCWEBMASTER@USGS.GOV

BONE DIGGER BONUS

BEST JOB ON EARTH

by Dr. Albert E. Sanders
Natural History Curator, Charleston Museum

A man and his son brought a fossil into my office for identification. As I was showing them some of the fossils in the preparation area, the man suddenly said, "You know, you have the best job in the world."

"Yes, I suppose I do" was my response.

This is not to say that there are no disappointments or frustrations in paleontology. Every profession has its share of ups and downs. But the excitement that one experiences in the discovery of new additions to the fossil record of a region more than makes up for any aggravations encountered along the way. When we excavate a new specimen, I am still impressed by the fact that as we slowly remove the dirt from around the bones, it is the first time they have seen the light of day in millions of years. Ours are the first human eyes ever to have seen them.

None of the many professional paleontologists that I know and work with has any regrets about entering the field, and I'm quite certain that virtually all of them would be dreadfully unhappy if, for some reason, they suddenly had to give up their abiding interest in fossils. If you are willing to obtain the proper education, I would say, "Do it!" You'll never get rich, but you certainly won't starve, either. There are many ways to measure wealth. Because I am doing the work I most enjoy, I consider myself to be as rich as any man on Earth.

FLINTSTONES BEDROCK CITY

This play area, campground, and theme park triad was inspired by the wildly popular *Flintstones* animated television series of the 1960s. From the Slidasaurus to the Brontoburgers, it's strictly fantasy, and only open from May to September. But it's a fun stop if you're touring South Dakota's dinosaur territories.

> U.S. Hwys. 16 and 385
> PO Box 649
> Custer, SD 57730
> (605) 673-4079
> Web site: http://www.flintstonesbedrockcity.com
> E-mail: NA

BLACK HILLS INSTITUTE OF GEOLOGICAL RESEARCH, INC.

Peter Larson is the heart and soul of South Dakota's Black Hills Institute. Perhaps most famous for the excavation—and subsequent federal abduction—of "Sue," the magnificent *Tyrannosaurus rex* now on display at Chicago's Field Museum, Larson is no less a wonder. No matter how many times he gets knocked down, he keeps getting up. And every time he does, there's another dinosaur discovery at his feet. He's golden when it comes to his first love—paleontology. And the fruits of his labor are on display at this rural museum.

> 217 Main St.
> Hill City, SD 57745
> (605) 574-4289

*Tyrannosaurus and
Euoplocephalus*

140

Web site: http://www.bhigr.com
E-mail: form on Web site

MAMMOTH SITE OF HOT SPRINGS, SD

Hundreds of woolly mammoths met their untimely death here, thanks to a slippery sinkhole during the Ice Age in South Dakota. Today, a mammoth-size bone bed is all that's left of their existence, but what a remarkable fossil find it turned out to be. The visitors center guides fossil fans through the history of the site and the beasts themselves. And educational outreach efforts bring the mammoths to classrooms all over the state.

1800 Hwy. 18 Bypass

PO Box 692

Hot Springs, SD 57747

(605) 745-6017

Web site: http://www.mammothsite.com

E-mail: mammoth@mammothsite.com

BADLANDS NATIONAL PARK

According to the National Park Service Web site, "Badlands National Park contains the world's richest Oligocene Epoch fossil beds, dating approximately 23 to 35 million years old. Scientists can study the evolution of mammal species such as the horse, sheep, rhinoceros, and pig in the Badlands formations." You can study those fossil riches, as well, as long as funding for the national park system doesn't go extinct.

25216 Ben Reifel Rd.

PO Box 6

Interior, SD 57750

(605) 433-5361

Web site: http://www.nps.gov/badl

E-mail: form on Web site

DINOSAUR PARK

According to the National Park Service, these concrete dinosaurs are terrific examples of roadside sculpture popular in the 1930s. Complete with picnic facilities, five or more of the "classics" still roam the hillsides of Rapid City, including *T. rex, Stegosaurus,* and *Apatosaurus*. Durable and photo-friendly, they're not science, but they *are* great fun.

940 Skyline Drive

Rapid City, SD 57702

Web site: NA

E-mail: NA

DINOSAURS IN CONCRETE

(Courtesy of the National Register of Historic Places/National Park Service, 1990)

Dinosaur Park is one of the most elaborate examples of roadside sculpture in the state of South Dakota and an excellent example of vernacular [native] public art. Mount Rushmore, about 20 miles southwest of Rapid City, became the site of the great carvings of four American presidents who played major roles in westward expansion. That sculpture was first dedicated in 1930, and by 1935, some 200,000 visitors had visited the unfinished monument. These statistics were not lost on the promoters of Rapid City. Tourism was big business, and the chamber of commerce was eager to make the connection between one successful sculpture and another.

The idea of dinosaurs as the subject of a new sculpture came from Dr. C. C. O'Hara, the retired president of the South Dakota School of Mines and a paleontologist who was fascinated by the prehistoric animal remains he had found in the Badlands of South Dakota. Others also liked the idea. The creation of concrete dinosaurs hit three nerves in the American aesthetic—a sense of the history of the West, an enjoyment of things larger than life, and a secret pleasure in being frightened. Dinosaur Park, located on a prominent hill above the town, was dedicated on May 22, 1936.

All five of the original dinosaurs were built in identical fashion. The frames are composed of 2-inch-diameter black iron pipe set in concrete. Around the central frame, body forms consist of a steel skeleton covered with wire mesh to which the concrete skin is applied. Oral tradition has it that the park's dinosaurs originally were gray, but today they are painted vivid green, with touches of pinkish red. Built to authentic size, the measurements of the five dinosaurs are as follows:

- *Triceratops—27 feet long, 11 feet high, 40-inch horns*
- *Tyrannosaurus rex—35 feet long, 16 feet high, 4-foot-long head*
- *"Brontosaurus" (now known as* Apatosaurus*)—80 feet long, 28 feet high*
- *Stegosaurus—11 feet long, 7 feet high*
- *"Trachodon" (now known as* Edmontosaurus*)—33 feet long, 17 feet 6 inches high.*

The "Brontosaurus," the largest of the dinosaurs, is visible for many miles and has become a local landmark.

Tyrannosaurus rex

SOUTH DAKOTA MUSEUM OF GEOLOGY

A truly extensive collection of dinosaurs, marine reptiles, flying reptiles, and other invertebrate fossils is housed, protected, and exhibited by this teaching museum in Rapid City. Included are (take a deep breath, it's a long list): the hadrosaur *Edmontosaurus, Triceratops, Tyrannosaurus rex, Iguanodon, Pachycephalosaurus,* mosasaurs, plesiosaurs, fossil fish, turtles, *Pteranodon,* and the flightless bird *Hesperornis.* Also at the museum are plant and small marine fossils, as well as insects.

South Dakota School of Mines and Technology

501 E. Saint Joseph St.

Rapid City, SD 57701

(605) 394-2467

Web site: http://museum.sdsmt.edu

E-mail: NA

WALL DRUG STORE DINOSAUR

Stretching your legs is more than a little fun when you're strolling through the legendary Wall Drug Store in Wall, South Dakota. First and foremost, there is the famous 80-foot dinosaur at the store's entrance, complete with picnic area and playground. But Wall Drug Store is more than *just* a dinosaur parking spot. It's a family business that started simply in the 1930s, only to evolve into a middle-American oasis and tourist haven. Everything from food to trinkets can be found there now. It's something you have to see to completely believe.

510 Main St.

Wall, SD 57790

(605) 279-2175

Web site: http://www.walldrug.com

E-mail: info@walldrug.com

SOUTH DAKOTA GEOLOGICAL SURVEY
AKELEY-LAWRENCE SCIENCE CENTER, USD
414 E. CLARK ST.
VERMILLION, SD 57069
(605) 677-5227
WEB SITE: HTTP://WWW.SDGS.USD.EDU
E-MAIL: DILES@USD.EDU (DERRIC ILES, STATE GEOLOGIST)

COON CREEK SCIENCE CENTER

Say "Gulf of Mexico" in the new millennium and you might picture the east coast of Texas, Louisiana, or Mississippi, perhaps. Now say "Gulf of Mexico" and rocket back in time 70 million years, and warm water covers most of western Tennessee. The Coon Creek Science Center helps students explore life beneath that prehistoric ocean through clam, snail, crab, shark, and mosasaur fossils. The science center is not a museum but an educational outreach facility that can be toured by organized groups by appointment only. But if your group is headed for McNairy County, Tennessee, it's a fossil find you shouldn't miss. For more information, or to set up a visit, call or write the following address:

Pink Palace Family of Museums
3050 Central Ave.
Memphis, TN 38111
(901) 320-6320
Web site: http://www.memphismuseums.org/creek.htm
E-mail: more_info@memphismuseums.org

GRAY FOSSIL SITE AND VISITORS CENTER

Tennessee governor Don Sundquist committed $8 million to the creation of a visitors center at the Gray Fossil Site on September 26, 2001. Rich with 7-to-4.5-million-year-old Miocene-Pliocene fossil deposits (the only find of this age ever unearthed in Appalachia), the Gray Fossil Site was discovered when road crews worked to reconstruct State Route 75. Governor Sundquist's 50,000-square-foot visitors center will house exhibits explaining the ancient Tennessee past, a fossil prep lab, an education center for school field trips and student enrichment, and a workshop for fossil fans. East Tennessee State University will supervise and direct the center and the fossil site.

c/o Friends of the Gray Fossil Site
State Rte. 75
PO Box 792
Dandridge, TN 37725
Web site: http://www.geocities.com/graysitefriends
E-mail: LAWhittemore@aol.com

Gallimimus

Albertosaurus

BONE DIGGER BONUS

COON CREEK'S KING

by Bobby King
Coon Creek Science Center

I have always been intrigued by Earth's prehistoric life. And the only means we have of studying that life is through a detailed examination of the fossil record. Through that study, we are given a window into Earth's ancient history.

The pinnacle of my career with the Coon Creek Science Center came in November 1990, as staff from our center and the Memphis Pink Palace Museum excavated the partial skeletal remains of a mosasaur. To see the ancient swimming reptile slowly uncovered and moved from its 70-million-year-old resting place is beyond description. This creature, at the top of the food chain, roamed western Tennessee during the Late Cretaceous Period.

Just as exciting, but in a different way, is the unique opportunity I have to share my experiences with the students who visit our center. To see their excitement and to help kindle the flame of curiosity in these young minds is compensation enough for the work I do. And my advice to them is always the same: Dare to dream, then nurture your dreams with diligent study and hard work.

That's my advice for you, too.

HANDS ON! REGIONAL MUSEUM

When kids slip into the Think Tank, they can explore a modest collection of dinosaur bones. But that's not the only prehistoric option open at the Hands On! Regional Museum. Traveling dinosaur exhibits like Kokoro's robotic dino show, Feathered Dinosaurs: The Avian Connection, are welcomed to the museum on a regular basis. So if you're in Johnson City, be sure to look into what fossil surprises might be in store.

315 E. Main St.
Johnson City, TN 37601
(423) 434-4263
Web site: http://www.handsonmuseum.org
E-mail: handson@handsonmuseum.org

FRANK H. McCLUNG MUSEUM

In August 2002, the rich prehistoric fossil legacy of the state was revealed in the Geology and the Fossil History of Tennessee exhibit at this university museum. Featuring underwater marine life common to prehistoric Tennessee, as well as a meat-eating *Albertosaurus* from nearby Alabama, carbon-forest botanical fossils, insects, and ancient mammals and alligators from the Gray Fossil Site in Washington County—as well as the only dinosaur ever discovered in the state: a plant-eating hadrosaur—it is one of the state's most comprehensive paleontology experiences.

University of Tennessee

1327 Circle Park Dr.

Knoxville, TN 37996

(865) 974-2144

Web site: http://mcclungmuseum.utk.edu

E-mail: museum@utk.edu

MEMPHIS PINK PALACE MUSEUM

You'll find dinosaur fossils and lifelike models in this—the biggest hands-on museum in the entire Southeast—featuring the Geology, 4.6 Billion Years of Earth History exhibit. Dinosaur tracks, a mastodon skeleton, a mosasaur, a *Dilophosaurus* model, and more prehistoric resources are all on display, along with exhibits on the Piggly Wiggly grocery chain, the American Civil War, Spanish explorers, and other important historic topics that impacted the state of Tennessee.

3050 Central Ave.

Memphis, TN 38111

(901) 320-6320

Web site: http://www.memphismuseums.org/museum.htm

E-mail: more_info@memphismuseums.org

TENNESSEE RIVER MUSEUM

From riverbank gun battles to steamboat adventures, life on the river is the primary theme of the Tennessee River Museum. But displays on archaeology and paleontology round out the modest exhibits.

507 Main St.

Savannah, TN 38372

(800) 552-3866

(901) 925-2364

Web site: NA

E-mail: NA

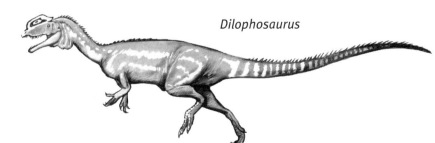

Dilophosaurus

TEXAS

AUSTIN NATURE AND SCIENCE CENTER DINO PIT

This outdoor dig simulation and play area was designed to give ordinary kids a taste of what it's like to look for and find prehistoric fossils. Dinosaur tracks, a field collection display—including fossil casts of specimens found nearby—an 8-foot-by-6-foot mammoth rib cage cast in bronze, and an observation deck are only part of what you'll find on-site. Fossils to be unearthed include fragments of mastodon, saber-toothed cat, giant tortoise, *Alamosaurus, Quetzalcoatlus, Tyrannosaurus rex,* mosasaur, plesiosaur, starfish, ammonites, and more.

> 301 Nature Center Dr.
> Austin, TX 78746
> (512) 327-8181
> Web site: http://www.ci.austin.tx.us/ansc
> E-mail: form on Web site

HARTMAN PREHISTORIC GARDEN

When 100-million-year-old *Ornithomimus*-like dinosaur tracks and other pre-historic fossils were found in this lush Austin location, the Zilker Botanical

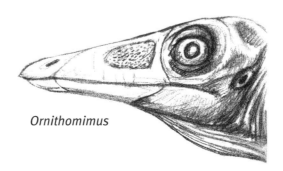

Ornithomimus

147

Gardens transformed the space into the Hartman Prehistoric Garden. Reproductions of the excavated tracks have been installed, along with a dinosaur model, and a waterfall, pond, and bog to simulate the dinosaur's prehistoric habitat. This is a beautiful dinosaur stop even Grandma will enjoy.

> Zilker Botanical Gardens/Austin Area Garden Center
> 2220 Barton Springs Rd.
> Austin, TX 78746
> (512) 477-8672
> Web site: http://www.zilkergarden.org
> E-mail: webmaster@zilkergarden.org

TEXAS MEMORIAL MUSEUM

This university museum recently shifted to an almost entirely natural science collection, including so many fossil treasures it's hard to describe them in a brief passage. Natural Wonders is an exhibit that highlights fossils from every prehistoric era. From dragonflies to dinosaur tracks to enormous flying pterosaurs, this Austin museum has it all—and rotates its exhibit specimens regularly. So if you go in June, you may see an entirely different selection of fossils than if you go again in October. It is an exceptional fossil outing on every level.

> 2400 Trinity St.
> Austin, TX 78705
> (512) 471-1604
> Web site: http://www.tmm.utexas.edu
> E-mail: form on Web site

BIG BEND NATIONAL PARK

On the Mexican-U.S. border, Big Bend National Park is 801,000 acres of west Texas diversity. The park is famous for many fossil finds, including the discovery in 1971 of *Quetzalcoatlus,* a massive flying reptile with a 35-foot wingspan. Smaller specimens have been found since then, but none to compare with this incredible giant. A fossil cast is on display at the visitors center. Another giant—the sauropod *Alamosaurus*—is known from Big Bend National Park, with an exceptionally large specimen of this dinosaur found in 1999. Super crocs like *Deinosuchus* have also been found at the park. It's a fabulous fossil destination for people who like to play outdoors.

> PO Box 129
> Big Bend National Park, TX 79834
> (432) 477-2251

Web site: http://www.nps.gov/bibe
E-mail: form on Web site

PANHANDLE-PLAINS HISTORICAL MUSEUM

The Texas panhandle has a rich history—from warring Comanches to oil wells to ancient fossils. This museum explores all those topics, and more. The paleontology and geology exhibits include a mounted *Allosaurus,* a *Triceratops* skull, a mastodon, a saber-toothed cat, and more.

2503 Fourth Ave.

Canyon, TX 79015

(806) 651-2244

Web site: http://www.panhandleplains.org

E-mail: gcvanderpool@pphm.wtamu.edu (Guy C. Vanderpool,
museum director)

DINOSAUR WORLD

Located near San Antonio, Dinosaur World (according to its Web site) "is like a museum and retail store in one. Throughout our store you will see life-size replicas of dinosaur and prehistoric animal skulls, teeth, claws, and bones. In Dinosaur World, you can buy the things you see and take home a piece of our prehistoric past! We sell fossils, mineral specimens, unique gifts, fossil reproductions, and educational products for young people. Our store was created to advance young people's education in science and paleontology." No admission is charged—of course—but you could walk out with substantially less cash after you see the fossils up for sale. Amazing! The store also sponsors lectures, field trips, and educator workshops.

8519 Blanco Rd.

Castle Hills, TX 78216

(210) 798-6224

Web site: http://www.dinosaurworld.com

E-mail: form on Web site

BRAZOSPORT MUSEUM OF NATURAL SCIENCE

Known primarily for its extensive collection of Gulf Coast seashells—the largest collection in the southern United States—the museum also features the lovely Dinosaur Island exhibit, where you'll see an *Allosaurus* skeleton, a reconstruction model of a sail-backed prehistoric reptile, and dozens of fossil specimens in cases. The museum will also help visitors identify fossils and shells of their own.

400 College Blvd.
Clute, TX 77531
(979) 265-7831
Web site: http://www.bcfas.org
E-mail: bmns@bcfas.org

CORPUS CHRISTI MUSEUM OF SCIENCE AND HISTORY

In addition to a fun paleontology hall with multiple fossil cases—including a *T. rex* skull, a pterosaur model, a mosasaur, dinosaur tracks, and a dinosaur nest—there are half a dozen other kid-friendly exhibits on display at this very engaging family museum. Don't miss Shipwreck!—a simulation of a Spanish treasure-ship run aground at Padre Island in 1554—or the Mitchell Campbell Wommack Reptiles of South Texas, with live snakes, turtles, lizards, and alligators in a museum ecosystem.

1900 N. Chaparral St.
Corpus Christi, TX 78401
(361) 826-4650
Web site: http://www.ccmuseum.com
E-mail: bonniel@cctexas.com

DALLAS MUSEUM OF NATURAL HISTORY

Dallas is one of the biggest cities in Texas, and the Dallas Museum of Natural History has some of the biggest fossil exhibits in the state. Permanent exhibits include a paleontology lab as well as the exhibits Ice Age Dallas, Texas Dinosaurs (including *Tenontosaurus*—a 120-million-year-old plant-eater discovered in the state in 1962), and perhaps its most distinctive dinosaur exhibit, Chromosaurs—amazing life-size dinosaur models made entirely of chrome automobile bumpers! This museum is too good to miss. And the Web site is almost as good as the museum itself. Check it out.

3535 Grand Ave.
Dallas, TX 75210
(214) 421-3466
Web site: http://www.dallasdino.org
E-mail: info@dmnhnet.org

THE SCIENCE PLACE

The Robo-Dino Gallery in the Dino Dig area features three robotic dinosaurs and a hydraulic dinosaur skeleton to help visitors understand how the robotics

BONE DIGGER BONUS

CHROMOSAUR CITY

(Courtesy of the Dallas Museum of Natural History)

Dinosaurs are stacked "bumper to bumper" on the grounds of the Dallas Museum of Natural History. No, they are not stuck in a long line of traffic. They are "Chromosaurs," dinosaur replicas made entirely of chrome automobile bumpers! Sculptor Jack Kearney created the life-size replica dinosaurs, including a T. rex towering 20 feet, and Triceratops and Stegosaurus sculptures that each stretch over 32 feet long. The Chromosaurs' similarity to their prehistoric counterparts is quite convincing. Collectively, the Chromosaur Collection weighs over 7 tons and took three years to complete.

Kearney is renowned for his bumper sculpture art, which, he says, happened purely by accident. In the early 1950s, he and his sculptor friends were roaming salvage yards in search for unique materials. "When we arrived at one of the dumps, I happened to notice a pile of automobile bumpers that were old and in poor condition," Kearney said. "I took a whole load to my house and tossed them on the grass. They accidentally fell into the shape of a ballet dancer."

Newly inspired, Kearney premiered his newfound art form in the mid 1950s with a show in New York entitled Alphabet Zoo, which consisted of twenty-six bumper sculpture animals arranged in alphabetical order, from anteater to zebra.

Today, Kearney's bumper sculptures can be seen in private and public collections across the country. They are familiar sights in his adopted home of Chicago. A replica African elephant stands in Lincoln Park Zoo and a tribute to the Tin Man from The Wizard of Oz can be seen in the city's Oz Park.

The Chromosaur Collection has been on loan to the Dallas Museum of Natural History since 1998 and is displayed on the museum grounds.

Allosaurus

work. Dozens of other exhibits and a giant IMAX theater make this a great family stop, no matter what kind of science you fancy.

Main Bldg.
1318 Second Ave.
Dallas, TX 75210
(214) 428-5555
Web site: http://www.scienceplace.org
E-mail: tellus@scienceplace.org

SHULER MUSEUM OF PALEONTOLOGY

Not only does this teaching museum house a wealth of dinosaur discoveries and a state-of-the-art fossil prep lab, it helps create exhibits for other museums as well. Lone Star Dinosaurs was a traveling exhibit created in partnership with the Fort Worth Museum of Science and History. Inspired in part by Dr. Louis Jacobs's book *Lone Star Dinosaurs,* the exhibit helped bring dinosaurs to museums that might not have otherwise experienced them.

Department of Geological Sciences
Southern Methodist University
Dallas, TX 75275
(214) 768-2750
Web site: http://www.geology.smu.edu/~vineyard/shulermus.html
E-mail: geol@mail.smu.edu

CENTENNIAL MUSEUM

According to its Web site, "The paleontology exhibit in the William Strain Room features invertebrate fossils from the surrounding mountains and vertebrate fossils from the El Paso region Ice Age."

University of Texas at El Paso
500 W. University Ave.
El Paso, TX 79968
(915) 747-5565
Web site: http://www.utep.edu/museum
E-mail: museum@utep.edu

FORT WORTH MUSEUM OF SCIENCE AND HISTORY

This award-winning hands-on museum is known for its creative, educational exhibits. Several of those top-notch displays involve local paleontology. The Lone Star Dinosaurs exhibit is 2,200 square feet of exploration, including real fossils and fossil casts of dinosaurs and other ancient reptiles native to Texas. *Acrocanthosaurus, Pleurocoelus, Tenontosaurus,* and *Tyrannosaurus rex,* as well as phytosaurs, hypsilophodonts, nodosaurs, hadrosaurs, and pterosaurs, are all part of the display, along with dinosaur egg clutches and more. Based in large part on the work of SMU paleontologist Dr. Louis Jacobs, the exhibit opened on July 4, 1997. And don't miss the working Dino Dig while you're there. It's a get-down-and-dirty way to learn about finding fossils.

> 1501 Montgomery St.
> Fort Worth, TX 76107
> (888) 255-9300
> (817) 255-9300
> Web site: http://www.fwmuseum.org
> E-mail: webmaster@fwmsh.org

DINOSAUR VALLEY STATE PARK

In 1909, a young girl walking down the path of the Paluxy River stumbled upon some strange impressions in the stony banks of the waterway. Friends and family told her they were marks made by Native Americans, but she didn't believe it. Years later, famed dinosaur tracker Roland T. Bird proved she was right when he confirmed the impressions were tracks left behind 100 million years before the little girl had been born. Dinosaur Valley State Park was built in honor and in preservation of those sauropod tracks, as well as the meat-eater tracks found nearby. Today, two other monuments to dinosaur history are also on display at the park—a *Tyrannosaurus rex* model and an *Apatosaurus* model originally created for the Sinclair Oil exhibit at the 1964–1965 World's Fair in New York City.

> Park Rd. 59
> PO Box 396
> Glen Rose, TX 76043
> (254) 897-4588
> Web site: http://www.tpwd.state.tx.us/park/dinosaur
> E-mail: form on Web site

HOUSTON MUSEUM OF NATURAL SCIENCE

Along with special temporary exhibits like National Geographic's SuperCroc, the HMNS has a permanent exhibit that examines the 3.5-billion-year history of life on Earth. "The museum's Hall of Paleontology contains more than 450 fossils and fossil replicas," according to the Web site. "From the humble trilobite to the mighty *Tyrannosaurus rex,* this exhibit hall will bring you face to face with the creatures that once ruled our planet."

1 Hermann Circle Dr.
Houston, TX 77030
(713) 639-4629
Web site: http://www.hmns.org
E-mail: webmaster@hmns.org

ROBERT A. VINES ENVIRONMENTAL SCIENCE CENTER

Robert Vines was a kind of traveling science teacher in 1950s Houston. He moved from school to school, trying to excite young people about the wonders of natural science. The creative science center named for that educator includes a Hall of Geology with a great collection of dinosaur and other prehistoric fossils. There's also a Hall of Oceanography and a Hall of Exotic Animals. Advance reservations are required to explore the center, so call ahead.

8856 Westview Dr.
Houston, TX 77055
(713) 365-4175
Web site: http://www.springbranchisd.com/instruc/science/vsc/
    missionhistory.htm
E-mail: vsc@springbranchisd.com

MUSEUM OF TEXAS TECH UNIVERSITY

This university museum was formed to help teach students to become expert museum staffers. The Natural Science Research Lab includes some dinosaur and prehistoric mammal fossil resources.

Fourth St. and Indiana Ave.
Box 43191
Lubbock, TX 79409
(806) 742-2490
Web site: http://www.depts.ttu.edu/museumttu
E-mail: museum.texastech@ttu.edu

HEARD NATURAL SCIENCE MUSEUM AND WILDLIFE SANCTUARY

A very modest selection of prehistoric fossils, including a mosasaur (*Tylosaurus*) skull and other trace fossils, is on display at this small-town museum.

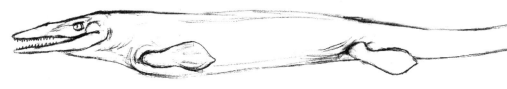

Tylosaurus

1 Nature Pl.
McKinney, TX 75069
(972) 562-5566
Web site: http://www.heardmuseum.org
E-mail: info@heardmuseum.org

DINOSAUR GARDENS

A wooded path 1,000 feet long is home to more than half a dozen prehistoric animal sculptures, including a *T. rex,* a saber-toothed cat, a *Dimetrodon,* and a *Triceratops.* (Look, too, for dinosaur trackways in the region.) Closed in the winter months.

(near U.S. 59 and FM 62)
Moscow, TX 75960
Web site: NA
E-mail: NA

WITTE MUSEUM

The museum's Dinosaur Gallery includes casts of a *Triceratops* and a *Tyrannosaurus rex* skeleton, *Edmontosaurus* skulls, a cross section of dinosaur teeth, and dinosaur-track casts gathered in Glen Rose.

3801 Broadway
San Antonio, TX 78209
(210) 357-1900
Web site: http://www.wittemuseum.org
E-mail: reservations@wittemuseum.org

MAYBORN MUSEUM (FORMERLY CALLED THE STRECKER)

Though this Lone Star State museum has long had fossil exhibits, including *Acrocanthosaurus* tracks and a 12-foot-long *Protostega* (a sea turtle), it *really* hit pay dirt with the discovery in 1978 of the Waco Mammoth Site. Today, more than twenty-four mammoths have been recovered from this bone bed, killed and preserved by what scientists believe was a single catastrophic event.

Mayborn Museum Complex (featuring the Strecker Collection)
1300 S. University-Parks
Waco, TX 76706
(254) 710-1110
Web site: http://www.baylor.edu/mayborn
E-mail: form on Web site

UTAH

THE DINOSAUR MUSEUM

If you visit only one dinosaur stop in Utah, make it the remarkable Dinosaur Museum in Blanding. Created by dinosaur experts Steven and Sylvia Czerkas, it clearly exhibits the complete history of the world of the dinosaurs. Because the Czerkases are paleontologists as well as fine sculptors, the exhibits—everything from skeletons to fossilized skin to fleshed-out models—are of top quality, scientifically and aesthetically. Don't miss the special exhibit of dinosaur eggs from around the world, featuring baby *Protoceratops* and *Maiasaura* sculptures.

> 754 S. 200 W.
> Blanding, UT 84511
> (435) 678-3454
> Web site: http://www.dinosaur-museum.org
> E-mail: dinos@dinosaur-museum.org

MUSEUM OF THE SAN RAFAEL

Utah is chock-full of dinosaur fossils, and even this small museum in Castle Dale reaps the benefits. In the William Lee Stokes Hall alone, you'll find an *Allosaurus,* a *Chasmosaurus,* the skull of a *Tyrannosaurus rex,* and replicas of fossilized eggs believed to contain dinosaur embryos.

> 96 N. 100 E.
> Castle Dale, UT 84513

(435) 381-5252
Web site: http://www.museumsanrafael.org
E-mail: info@museumsanrafael.org

DINOSAUR NATIONAL MONUMENT

While this site's mailing address is in Colorado, the actual monument is in Utah. Literally hundreds of dinosaur skeletons were preserved in the sediments of an ancient riverbed, only to be discovered 145 million years later. The dinosaur quarry of Dinosaur National Monument yielded hundreds of individuals and dozens of species, including plant-eaters like *Apatosaurus, Diplodocus,* and *Stegosaurus,* and meat-eaters like *Allosaurus*. Don't miss the visitors center. And contact the Chamber of Commerce in Vernal, Utah, for information about the dates and events scheduled for the region's annual Dinosaur Days.

4545 E. Hwy. 40

Dinosaur, CO 81610

(970) 374-3000

Web site: http://www.nps.gov/dino

E-mail: form on Web site

TOPAZ MOUNTAIN ROCKHOUND RECREATION AREA

In the mood to collect topaz, crystals, geodes, and prehistoric trilobites? Check out the rustic trails of the Topaz Mountain Rockhound Recreation Area. There are no facilities—no bathrooms or tour guides—but there are resources you can collect and keep. It's an exciting fossil stop in the heart of southern Utah.

(55 miles west of Delta via U.S. Hwy. 6 and paved county road)

Fillmore Field Office/Bureau of Land Management

35 E. 500 N.

Fillmore, UT 84631

(435) 743-3100

Web site: http://www.recreation.gov/detail.cfm?ID=2214

E-mail: SMaurer@plia.org

GRAND STAIRCASE-ESCALANTE NATIONAL MONUMENT

Layer upon layer of geologic history is blanketed across the landscape of the Grand Staircase-Escalante National Monument. And for decades, paleontological teams have tried to gently fold back the covers to reveal what lies underneath. A few layers down, you find prehistoric animals that thrived during a recent Ice Age. Down a few *more* layers, you find dinosaurs (including duckbilled hadrosaurs with well-preserved fossilized skin). And beneath the dinosaurs are layers with even more ancient reptiles and amphibians, including marine animals that swam in a tropical sea. Collecting fossils without a permit is illegal on these federal grounds, but looking for fossils to report to park staff is perfectly fine.

190 E. Center

Kanab, UT 84741

(435) 644-4300

Web site: http://www.ut.blm.gov/monument

E-mail: escalante_interagency@blm.gov

DAN O'LAURIE MUSEUM

This small natural science and history museum offers a nice sampling of dinosaur fossils native to the Moab, Utah, region, including tracks and a femur. It also has artifacts and tools made by ancient peoples like the Anasazi and the Fremont.

118 E. Center St.

Moab, UT 84532

(435) 259-7985

Web site: http://www.moab-utah.com/danolaurie/museum.html

E-mail: NA

MILL CANYON DINOSAUR TRAIL

If you're an outdoorsy fossil fan, the Mill Canyon Dinosaur Trail may be exactly your cup of tea. Just a quarter of a mile long, this "outdoor museum" reveals millions of years of fossil evidence in the ground, right where it started. A sign marks the start and explains, "This self-guided trail contains 150-million-year-old skeletal remains of numerous kinds of dinosaurs, including *Allosaurus, Camptosaurus, Stegosaurus,* and *Camarasaurus*. It also contains petrified wood." It goes on to explain that while there are no guards,

Ceratosaurus

respectful visitors will obey the law and leave fossil treasures where they find them for the next visitor. Bureau of Land Management law-enforcement officers patrol the region regularly and will prosecute violators.

(U.S. Hwy. 191, mile marker 141)

Moab Field Office

82 E. Dogwood

Moab, UT 84532

(435) 259-2100

Web site: http://www.ugs.state.ut.us/utahgeo/dinofossil dinotracks.htm (Utah Geological Survey—some details)

E-mail: christinewilkerson@utah.gov (Christine Wilkerson, UGS dinosaur-track expert)

POISON SPIDER MESA DINOSAUR TRACKS

Literature mentions sauropod trackways on Potash Road. Visitors who have made the journey say, "Remember Poison Spider Mesa," the destination marker that makes the weathered slab of tracks possible to find. It's a small return on a significant driving effort, but if you're in Moab, it might be worth the drive. For a detailed map, contact the local Bureau of Land Management. And, again, fossil collection is prohibited and will be prosecuted.

(aka Potash Road Dinosaur Tracks)

(4 miles north of Moab, on Hwy. 191 to Potash Rd.)

Moab Field Office

82 E. Dogwood

Moab, UT 84532

(435) 259-2100

Web site: http://www.ugs.state.ut.us/utahgeo/dinofossil/ dinotracks.htm (Utah Geological Survey—some details)

E-mail: christinewilkerson@utah.gov (Christine Wilkerson, UGS dinosaur-track expert)

GEORGE S. ECCLES DINOSAUR PARK

Imagine you've somehow rocketed back in time to a beautiful place where dinosaurs roam free. It might look something like this wonderful dinosaur park, about an hour north of Salt Lake City in Ogden. Dozens of dinosaur models are scattered across the 5-acre river parkway landscape—well over one hundred in all. Though some species are central to Utah, like *Utahraptor,* all are of interest to dinosaur enthusiasts. Look for *Triceratops, Maiasaura, Tyrannosaurus rex, Parasaurolophus, Ceratosaurus, Camptosaurus, Allosaurus, Diplodocus, Amargasaurus, Baryonyx, Torvosaurus, Chasmosaurus,* and much, *much* more.

1544 E. Park Blvd.

Ogden, UT 84401

(801) 393-3466

Web site: http://www.dinosaurpark.org

E-mail: dinosaurpark@ci.ogden.ut.us

MUSEUM OF NATURAL SCIENCE

This wonderful museum of natural science includes fossil and dinosaur exhibits, both on campus and online. Look for *Allosaurus, Camptosaurus, Dimetrodon,* an ichthyosaur, and a saber-toothed cat.

Weber State University

Lind Lecture Hall

Ogden, UT 84408

(801) 626-6000

Web site: http://community.weber.edu/museum

E-mail: mediarelations@weber.edu

ESCALANTE PETRIFIED FOREST STATE PARK

Sixty to 70 million years ago, a lush tropical forest grew in what would eventually become Escalante, Utah. Dinosaurs thundered across the acres, nibbling the branches of great conifer trees—or the meaty flesh of one another. Millions of years later, the fossilized remains of those trees and dinosaurs can be found scattered about a well-marked interpretive trail at Escalante Petrified Forest State Park for visitors to see and enjoy.

(710 N. Reservoir Rd., off scenic byway 12)

Garfield County Tourism Office

55 S. Main

Panguitch, UT 84759

(800) 444-6689

(435) 676-1160

Web site: http://www.brycecanyoncountry.com/petrified.html

E-mail: travgar@color-country.net

Utahraptors and Gastonia

160

CLEVELAND-LLOYD DINOSAUR QUARRY

In 1928, fossil hounds discovered this exceptional bone bed that's yielded a tangle of 10,000 different Jurassic dinosaur bone pieces—enough to build a number of composite dinosaur skeletons for museum display. Even today— more than seventy-five years later—the beds produce scientifically significant dinosaur fossils. *Allosaurus* is one of the dinosaur types commonly found in the Cleveland-Lloyd quarry, but a number of other species have also been identified. A juvenile *Allosaurus* is mounted in the visitors center and dis- played with cases of other fossils against a mural of prehistoric life from 147 million years ago.

> Bureau of Land Management Price Field Office
>
> 125 S. 600 W.
>
> Price, UT 84501
>
> (435) 636-3600
>
> Web site: http://www.blm.gov/utah/price/quarry.htm
>
> E-mail: webmaster@blm.gov

COLLEGE OF EASTERN UTAH PREHISTORIC MUSEUM

Utah State paleontologist Jim Kirkland helps Don Burge keep this teaching museum top-notch. Located in the heart of Utah's dinosaur country, it fea- tures two prehistoric halls. Dinosaur fans will want to head straight for the Hall of Dinosaurs and Kirkland's own discovery, *Utahraptor*. But they'll also enjoy the museum's mascot, "Al"—an *Allosaurus*. Plant-eating *Camptosaurus, Camarasaurus, Chasmosaurus, Gastonia, Parasaurolophus,* and *Stegosaurus* are also on display, along with dozens of other fossil gems.

> 155 E. Main St.
>
> Price, UT 84501
>
> (800) 817-9949
>
> (435) 613-5060
>
> Web site: http://museum.ceu.edu
>
> E-mail: shawna.carroll@ceu.edu (Shawna Carroll,
>
>   director of education)

EARTH SCIENCE MUSEUM

"Dinosaur" Jim Jensen had a knack for finding dinosaur fossils—such a knack that he excavated more dinosaur bones than he had space to warehouse them for many years. A temporary storage space under the Brigham Young University athletic stadium bleachers housed some of the fossil treasures for a time, but today Jensen's best discoveries are on display in the BYU Earth Science Museum (as are finds collected by other paleontologists who have followed in his footsteps). Included are skeletal mounts of *Camptosaurus, Stegosaurus, Allosaurus,* and the sail-backed reptile *Dimetrodon;* a *Tyrannosaurus rex* skull; a lovely mural of Jurassic Utah; as well as dinosaur eggs, prehistoric mammals, a prep lab, touch tables, and much, *much* more. Viewed by appointment only. This is well worth the trip.

Brigham Young University

1683 N. Canyon Rd.

PO Box 23300

Provo, UT 84602

(801) 378-3680

Web site: http://cpms.byu.edu/ESM/index.html

E-mail: ken_stadtman@byu.edu (Ken Stadtman, curator)

WASHINGTON COUNTY TRACKSITES

Utah Geological Survey dinosaur-track expert Christine Wilkerson compiled this list of Washington County (and other Utah) trackways on the UGS Web site. Included are approximate trackway locations, seasonal hours, fees (where fees apply), directions, and solid descriptions of what you can expect to see at each site. If you don't find what you want to know on the Web site itself, write to the address given below.

Dixie Resource Area/Bureau of Land Management

225 N. Bluff St.

St. George, UT 84770

(435) 673-4654

Web site: http://www.ugs.state.ut.us/utahgeo/dinofossil/
    dinotracks.htm (Utah Geographical Survey—some details)

E-mail: christinewilkerson@utah.gov

UTAH MUSEUM OF NATURAL HISTORY

Dinosaurs are central to Utah's geology, and Utah's geology is central to the Utah Museum of Natural History. More than fifty exhibits are dedicated to those prehistoric fossils, including Dinosaur Tales: The Science Behind the Stories, and dozens of family-oriented activities and lectures each year. It's an outstanding museum in the heart of the state capital.

University of Utah

1390 E. Presidents Circle

Salt Lake City, UT 84112

(801) 581-6927

Web site: http://www.umnh.utah.edu

E-mail: webmaster@umnh.utah.edu

RED FLEET STATE PARK

Two species of dinosaurs left more than 200 tracks along the shore of the Red Fleet Reservoir, roughly 10 miles north of Vernal, Utah, just off of U.S. Highway 191. Expect a 2-mile, round-trip hike during the summer. During winter months, snow may make it impossible to see the tracks.

8750 U.S. Hwy. 191

Vernal, UT 84078

(435) 789-4432

Web site: http://www.stateparks.utah.gov/park_pages/parkpage
.php?id=rfsp

E-mail: parkcomment@utah.gov

BONE DIGGER BONUS

MURDER IN JURASSIC PARK: THE CLEVELAND-LLOYD DINOSAUR QUARRY

by Terry Gates
Utah Museum of Natural History

Although the ratio of carnivores to herbivores there led researchers to conclude that the Cleveland-Lloyd Dinosaur Quarry in central Utah—one of the most famous dinosaur sites in the world—was a predator trap similar to the La Brea Tar Pits, a new study concludes that drought was the primary cause of death at this site.

The CLDQ site has yielded thousands of fossilized bones and preserves the remains of at least eleven different kinds of dinosaurs from the Late Jurassic.

Remarkably, the remains of dinosaur carnivores, or theropods, outnumber those of herbivores by about 3 to 1. The overwhelming majority of these fossils belong to a single species of large theropod, Allosaurus *fragilis. According to the predator-trap view, theropods were killed over many years while pursuing herbivorous dinosaurs such as* Stegosaurus *that got stuck in the mud.*

This new study, which involved the assessment of an array of potential hypotheses using a broad range of data sources, re-evaluated the genesis of the quarry. The data, derived from analyses of the entombing sediments and the fossils themselves, do not support the predator-trap scenario or various other hypotheses. Instead, several lines of evidence are most consistent with drought as the primary cause of death at CLDQ.

Drought has been implicated in a number of other Late Jurassic dinosaur quarries, and this study suggests that it may well have been the culprit at Cleveland-Lloyd as well.

UTAH FIELD HOUSE OF NATURAL HISTORY STATE MUSEUM

For decades, the Utah Field House was the permanent home of the Dinosaur Gardens, one of the most beautiful collections of concrete dinosaur sculptures in the United States, as well as a collection of fossils. In 2002, the Utah Field House closed to prepare for a new and improved museum that opened in the spring of 2004. Some of the same features were incorporated into the modern architecture and exhibit space, including many of the concrete dinosaurs. But crisp, updated fossil exhibits bring the old and the new together to make this a terrific Utah dinosaur stop of historic significance.

496 E. Main St.

Vernal, UT 84078

(435) 789-3799

Web site: http://www.stateparks.utah.gov/park_pages/field.htm

E-mail: utahfieldhouse@utah.gov

UTAH GEOLOGICAL SURVEY
1594 W. NORTH TEMPLE
PO BOX 146100
SALT LAKE CITY, UT 84114
(801) 537-3300
WEB SITE: HTTP://WWW.UGS.STATE.UT.US
E-MAIL: CHRISTINEWILKERSON@UTAH.GOV
(CHRISTINE WILKERSON, UGS DINOSAUR-TRACK EXPERT)

VERMONT

"CHAMP" OF LAKE CHAMPLAIN

For four centuries, people have reported seeing a plesiosaur-like animal (lovingly called "Champ" or "Champy") rise from the depths of Lake Champlain, a deep body of cold water that washes up against the shores of Canada, New York, and Vermont. Want to take a look for yourself? One of the best ways to do so is on the ferry provided (for a low fee) by Burton Island State Park in Vermont. For more information about the legend of Champ, see this exceptional Web site created by the folks at U-Haul—http://www.uhaul.com/supergraphics/champ.

Burton Island State Park

Box 123

St. Albans Bay, VT 05481

(802) 524-6353

Web site: http://www.vtstateparks.com/htm/burton.cfm

E-mail: parks@state.vt.us

CHAMP CHARTERS

Looking for Champ? Captain Paul H. Boileau is at your service. And while he doesn't promise you'll see the watery wonder, he does promise to share his Champ stories as you try.

78 Main St.

Burlington, VT 05401

(802) 864-3790

(802) 777-0940 (cellular boat phone)

Web site: http://www.champcharters.com

E-mail: info@champcharters.com

ECHO LEAHY CENTER

Looking for a little more information on Champ and the environment that inspired his legend? Visit the Echo Leahy Center's Before the Basin exhibit. As the Web site says, "Travel back in time to explore the world of the Champlain Valley when the Adirondack Mountains were as high as the Himalayas, or to the time when beluga whales and seals swam in the salty waters of the Champlain Sea."

Lake Aquarium and Science Center

1 College St.

Burlington, VT 05401

(802) 864-1848

Web site: http://www.echovermont.org

E-mail: info@echovermont.org

PERKINS GEOLOGY MUSEUM

The Perkins Museum of Geology has a one-room exhibit hall that explores the geology and paleo-past of the state and other global regions, including

"Charlotte," the Vermont whale—a prehistoric whale found during railroad construction between Rutland and Burlington, Vermont. (The Champlain Sea covered Vermont during Charlotte's prehistoric life span.)

Delehanty Hall
University of Vermont—Trinity Campus
180 Colchester Ave.
Burlington, VT 05405
(802) 656-8694
Web site: http://geology.uvm.edu/museumwww/intropage.html
    or http://www.uvm.edu/perkins
E-mail: NA

MONTSHIRE MUSEUM OF SCIENCE

Dozens of hands-on educational exhibits fill this museum of natural science, including an exhibit on fossils. "Feel for a hidden fossil," the Web site says, "and try to guess which photo matches it. Also see a fossil of a local dinosaur, *Coelophysis,* and touch the thighbone of an *Apatosaurus.*"

1 Montshire Rd.
Norwich, VT 05055
(802) 649-2200
Web site: http://www.montshire.net
E-mail: montshire@montshire.org

BONE DIGGER BONUS

When railroad workers hit bone while laying track in Vermont in 1849, they thought they'd hit a long-buried horse or the body of some other dearly departed piece of livestock. They were wrong. What they'd unearthed in the bogs of Charlotte, Vermont, were the fossilized bones of a 12,000-year-old beluga whale from the Pleistocene Epoch. But how did a whale end up buried in landlocked Vermont?

As the glaciers from the end of the last Ice Age melted back, the sea level rose and flooded the Champlain Valley. So, for a time, that part of Vermont was drowned under an arm of the sea. "Charlotte," the nickname experts gave this ancient cousin of the modern beluga whale, died in the shallows of that prehistoric sea and was fossilized long before she was discovered in 1849. Named the Vermont State Fossil in 1993, Charlotte is one of the only state fossils that still has living relatives thriving nearby.

VERMONT GEOLOGICAL SURVEY
103 S. MAIN ST., LOGUE COTTAGE
WATERBURY, VT 05671
(802) 241-3608
WEB SITE: HTTP://WWW.ANR.STATE.VT.US/DEC/GEO/VGS.HTM
E-MAIL: LAURENCE.BECKER@STATE.VT.US
(LAURENCE BECKER, STATE GEOLOGIST)

VIRGINIA

VIRGINIA TECH GEOLOGICAL SCIENCES MUSEUM

From 8 a.m. to 4 p.m., Monday through Friday, students and visitors can explore the Virginia Tech Geological Science Museum on the Blacksburg campus. According to the Web site, "On display are an extensive mineral collection, fossils, and area mining history exhibits. Admission to the museum is free, and it is regularly visited by citizens, visitors, students, and teachers from area schools at all levels."

Department of Geological Sciences

Virginia Polytechnic Institute and State University

4044 Derring Hall, Second Fl.

Blacksburg, VA 24061

(540) 231-6521

Web site: http://www.geol.vt.edu/outreach/museum.html

E-mail: geosciences@vt.edu

PALEOWORLD RESEARCH FOUNDATION

Though this complete paleo-experience is headquartered in Virginia, the real activity takes place in Montana, China, and other exotic dinosaur locales—because Paleoworld offers families the chance to dig for dinosaurs alongside scientific experts. There are plans for the Hell Creek Dinosaur Museum at some point in the not-so-distant future. But until those plans are solidified, look for great Web site dinosaur features and dig opportunities outside of Virginia.

12950 Freestone Ct.

Woodbridge, VA 22192

(941) 473-9511

Web site: http://www.paleoworld.org

E-mail: paleoworld@paleoworld.org

THE MUSEUM OF CULPEPER HISTORY

This museum of Virginia history explores many different aspects of the state, including 215-million-year-old dinosaur tracks—one of the largest trackways ever discovered. The Revolutionary War, the American Civil War, famous Virginians, and other fascinating subjects are also explored.

803 S. Main St.

Culpeper, VA 22701

(540) 829-1749

Web site: http://www.culpepermuseum.com

E-mail: contact@culpepermuseum.com

NATURAL TUNNEL STATE PARK

For more than one hundred years, fossil fans and students of the Ice Age have flocked to Natural Tunnel State Park to explore the bizarre geologic structure formed more than a million years ago during a glacial period. Groundwater rich in carbonic acid bubbled through rock crevices, dissolving limestone and dolomite bedrock to create an underground tunnel. Stock Creek has flowed through the stone tunnel for centuries, eroding stone to reveal prehistoric fossils in the walls. Fossils freed from the stony caverns are flushed through the rushing currents and deposited in creek beds downstream, where fossil collectors find them by the dozens. It's a truly unique fossil experience worth discovering.

Rte. 3, Box 250

Duffield, VA 24244

(276) 940-2674

Web site: http://www.recreation.gov/detail.cfm?ID=2310

E-mail: form on Web site

VIRGINIA MUSEUM OF NATURAL HISTORY

Fossils are only part of this museum dedicated to Virginia's natural history. Nevertheless, its large collections (11,500 invertebrate fossils, 1,200 plant fossils, and 5,000 vertebrate fossils) allow the museum to regularly rotate the selection on view. So visit the fossil displays often for a glimpse of something new.

1001 Douglas Ave.
Martinsville, VA 24112
(276) 666-8600
Web site: http://www.vmnh.net
E-mail: webmaster@vmnh.net

THE MUSEUM OF THE MIDDLE APPALACHIANS

Because so many Ice Age mammals have been unearthed in Saltville, it's not surprising that this history museum has exhibits on both Virginia geology and Ice Age animals common to the area. Look for a mastodon, a woolly mammoth, a musk ox, a black bear, a giant beaver, and other fossil traces in the paleontological exhibit. And be sure to explore the museum's summer dig workshops before you schedule your visit or vacation.

PO Box 910
Saltville, VA 24370
(276) 496-3633
Web site: http://www.museum-mid-app.org
E-mail: info@museum-mid-app.org

BONE DIGGER BONUS

EVOLUTION, VIRGINIA STYLE

by Dr. Nicholas C. Fraser
Virginia Museum of Natural History

Two unique sites in Virginia have paved the way for significant advances in our understanding of the evolution of land vertebrates. One, near Richmond, has yielded remains of a mammal-like reptile that was previously considered largely restricted to the southern hemisphere.

The second site contains exceptionally well-preserved plants, insects, fish, and reptiles. Among the insects are a number of very unusual forms that have not previously been described, including some of the world's first true flies.

I consider this site comparable to the famous Solnhofen localities (of Archaeopteryx *fame) in Germany, and it must rank among the most important fossil sites in North America.*

DINOSAUR LAND

For more than twenty-six years, the fiberglass dinosaurs (and cobras and King Kongs!) of Virginia's Dinosaur Land have thrilled young children and inspired them to dream really big, sometimes prehistoric, dreams. From 3 to 30 feet long, the models offer significant variety, even if the science is slightly off target. This is great Americana in an outdoor setting for the whole family.

3848 Stonewall Jackson Hwy.

White Post, VA 22663

(540) 869-2222

Web site: http://www.dinosaurland.com

E-mail: webmaster@dinosaurland.com

U.S. GEOLOGICAL SURVEY
VIRGINIA STATE MINERALS INFORMATION
984 NATIONAL CENTER
RESTON, VA 20192
(703) 648-4758
WEB SITE: HTTP://MINERALS.USGS.GOV/MINERALS/PUBS/STATE/VA.HTML
E-MAIL: ATANNER@USGS.GOV
(ARNOLD TANNER)

WASHINGTON

SUN LAKE-DRY FALLS STATE PARK

About 7 miles southwest of Coulee City, this site yielded fossils of a small Miocene rhinoceros. Today, an interpretive center—complete with a life-size model of the baby rhino—helps explain what the ancient world was like for that prehistoric mammal and why it's important to visitors today.

34875 Park Lake Rd.
Coulee City, WA 99115
(360) 902-8844
Web site: http://www.parks.wa.gov/parkpage.asp?selectedpark=
   Sun+Lakes
E-mail: infocent@parks.wa.gov

GINKGO PETRIFIED FOREST STATE PARK

According to the Washington State Parks and Recreation Web site, the park "was set aside as a historic preserve when remains of a fossil forest were unearthed during highway construction in the 1930s. Petrified wood from many different trees are common in the area, but specimens of petrified ginkgo are rare. Many buildings on the premises owe their origin to the work of the 1930s Civilian Conservation Corps." According to fossil fans who've made the journey, it's an astonishing look at the world as it used to be, thanks to a three-quarters-of-a-mile marked outdoor trail.

(approximately 30 miles east of Ellensburg, on the Columbia River)
(509) 856-2700
(360) 902-8844
Web site: http://www.parks.wa.gov/parkpage.asp?selectedpark=
   Ginkgo
E-mail: infocent@parks.wa.gov

THE JACKLIN COLLECTION

Thanks to the generosity of donors Lyle and Lela Jacklin, visitors to Washington State University in Pullman can explore specimens that include fossilized dinosaur bones, 12-million-year-old petrified wood, and 15-million-year-old petrified palm tree sections from within the state. For information or to arrange a tour, e-mail or telephone the Department of Geology. Also on campus is the Harold E. Culver Study Memorial, dedicated to geologist and former WSU geology professor Harold Eugene Culver and his loyal students, who donated more than one hundred amazing fossil specimens to the museum. Skulls of a saber-toothed cat known as *Smilodon,* a dire wolf, and a *Dimetrodon* are just a few of the wonderful items exhibited.

Smilodon

171

Harold E. Culver Study Memorial, Rm. 124
Webster Physical Sciences Bldg.
Department of Geology
PO Box 642812
Washington State University
Pullman, WA 99164
(509) 335-3009
Web site: http://www.wsu.edu:8080/~geology/museums/
   jacklin.html
E-mail: geology@wsu.edu

STONEROSE INTERPRETIVE CENTER AND EOCENE FOSSIL SITE

If you doubt a world of beauty existed before man strolled on the scene to appreciate it, think again. The Stonerose Interpretive Center reveals layers of flowers that were trapped between the volcanic ash spit out on the Washington landscape 50 million years ago during the Eocene Epoch, along with leaves, fish, and even prehistoric insects. After paying the admission fee and listening to a short lesson from the site's curator, visitors can dig for up to three specimens for their own private collections at the Boot Hill fossil site.

15-1 N. Kean St.
Republic, WA 99166
(509) 775-2295
Web site: http://www.stonerosefossil.org
E-mail: srfossils@rcabletv.com
Ferry County Web site: http://www.ferrycounty.com/stonerose
E-mail: editor@ferrycounty.com

BURKE MUSEUM OF NATURAL HISTORY AND CULTURE

Located near the Washington coast, this great natural history museum has exhibits that celebrate the grinding glaciers of the ancient Pacific Northwest and the dinosaurs that inhabited the western United States long before the Ice Age. As you walk through the Life and Times of Washington State exhibit, you'll be amazed by the fossils represented—everything from a *Stegosaurus* and an *Allosaurus* to a sea reptile called an elasmosaur, and so much in

Stegosaurus

between. Special classes for children bring the magic of dinosaurs to life. And you can explore the exhibit online before you go in person.

Box 353010
University of Washington
Seattle, WA 98195
(206) 543-5590
Web site: http://www.washington.edu/burkemuseum
E-mail: recept@u.washington.edu

PACIFIC SCIENCE CENTER

A dozen or more exciting regular exhibits make the Pacific Science Center one of the best hands-on museums in the country. But the exhibit Dinosaurs: A Journey Through Time makes it a great stop for this book's dinophile readers. Seven moving, growling robotic dinosaurs bring the Mesozoic Era back to life in Seattle. Don't miss the Insect Village or the Tropical Butterfly House while you're there.

200 Second Ave. N.
Seattle, WA 98109
(206) 443-2001
Web site: http://www.pacsci.org
E-mail: webmaster@pacsci.org

BONE DIGGER BONUS

FOSSIL FLOWERS IN THE EVERGREEN STATE

Imagine a place where you can gather 50-million-year-old plant and insect fossils alongside paleontologists and ordinary fossil fans. You've just pictured Stonerose in the town of Republic, Washington.

During the Eocene Epoch, Republic was part of an ancient lake, made mineral-rich and murky by the regular release of volcanic ash. When plants and insects slipped into the dark waters, they were often covered with fine, wet soil called sediment from the bottom of the lake. Over time, many of those ancient life-forms turned to fossils.

Now the bottom of the lake has turned into dry layers of stone called tuffaceous shale, which peel apart like the pages of an ancient book. Between the layers are what's left of those ancient plant and animal secrets. If you stop by the Stonerose Interpretive Center, you can buy an admission sticker to dig for and keep up to three fossils per day. But remember that if you find a rare specimen, the scientists at Stonerose will want to keep it to learn more about ancient life.

WEST VIRGINIA

WEST VIRGINIA STATE MUSEUM

Created at the turn of the twentieth century, this is a large historical museum with artifacts representing topics more political and cultural than scientific (i.e., Indian migration, the American Civil War, settlers' cabins, quilting displays). But there is a modest collection of fossils on permanent display, including a slab of prehistoric shale with the footprints of an unidentified ancient amphibian that predates the dinosaurs.

> 1900 Kanawha Blvd. E.
> Charleston, WV 25305
> (304) 558-0220
> Web site: http://www.wvculture.org/museum
> E-mail: jim.mitchell@wvculture.org (James Mitchell, curator)

BLUESTONE WILDLIFE MUSEUM

Not much of a Web site—just a photo and a general West Virginia museum contact e-mail, in fact. But the small museum in Hinton has a modest collection of local fossils along with exhibits centered on contemporary taxidermy.

> Rte. 87, Box 10
> Hinton, WV 25951
> (304) 558-0220, ext. 727

Web site: http://www.museumsofwv.org/museum.cfm?
    museum=25
E-mail: info@museumsofwv.org

WEST VIRGINIA FOSSIL CLUB

This very active club has regular meetings and fossil-finding field trips in and around West Virginia. If you plan to be in the area, check to see if you can join in the discovery.

908 Clark St.

Shinnston, WV 26431

(304) 592-5014

Web site: http://www.prehistoricplanet.com/wvfc

E-mail: caliban7@wvonline.net

BONE DIGGER BONUS

PREHISTORIC PLANTS

by Dr. George Deemings
Curator, West Virginia State Museum

West Virginia fossil geology dates to the Devonian, Mississippian, Pennsylvanian, and Pleistocene periods. The land that is now West Virginia was almost always covered by sea-water.

During the Devonian Period, plants colonized the land and flourished during the Mississippian and Pennsylvanian periods. Most of the great coal beds now found in West Virginia were laid down at that time.

Picture a shallow, swampy inland sea, heavy with humidity and rich in insect and plant life. Amphibians splash and vocalize in their eagerness to feed. Their fossil remains can commonly be found in streambeds and mine discard dumps known as "tailings" through-out West Virginia.

The West Virginia State Museum displays sections of fossilized plants such as Lepidodendron, Lycopodium, Calamites, Cordaites, *and seeded ferns. A large slab of shale displays the footprints of an unknown amphibian. Dioramas depict the periods responsible for the geology of the state.*

175

WISCONSIN

GEOLOGY MUSEUM

When this ambitious university museum decided it wanted to exhibit dinosaurs—creatures never found in Wisconsin—they went out into the Badlands and found some! In cooperation with the Black Hills Institute in South Dakota, they excavated two plant-eating hadrosaurs, keeping one as payment for the hard labor of recovering both. They later excavated a *Tyrannosaurus rex* skull, nodosaurs, *Triceratops,* and other dinosaur fragments on private lands in Montana, as well as other prehistoric creatures from additional locations. As a result, this small museum has first-class specimens—some of the best in the region, in fact.

University of Wisconsin—Madison

1215 W. Dayton St.

Madison, WI 53706

(608) 262-1412

Web site: http://www.geology.wisc.edu/~museum

E-mail: rich@geology.wisc.edu

MILWAUKEE PUBLIC MUSEUM

An ancient tropical sea teeming with life is one of the subjects covered in this hands-on museum's Streets of Old Milwaukee exhibit. Included in the look back is a glimpse of Wisconsin's prehistoric past. North America was covered by a shallow sea that was alive with marine creatures 425 million years ago, and the prehistoric diorama within the Streets exhibit explores that ancient sea. You'll find dinosaur exhibits as well, including what they call the "largest known dinosaur skull" and a life-size replica of *Tyrannosaurus rex*.

800 W. Wells St.
Milwaukee, WI 53233
(414) 278-2702
Web site: http://www.mpm.edu
E-mail: NA

INTERSTATE STATE PARK

During the Wisconsin Ice Age, prehistoric mammals ruled the land. This hands-on center helps visitors understand that transition and the animals that survived—and then slipped into extinction. And thanks to the Junior Ranger and Wisconsin Explorer programs, kids of all ages who visit the center receive a free "discovery booklet." Finish half the fossil-oriented activities in it and you'll win an award and iron-on Junior Ranger patch. Don't miss the 20-minute video on the Wisconsin Ice Age.

BONE DIGGER BONUS

IMPORTED DUCKBILL, ANYONE?

Although the University of Wisconsin's Geology Museum had possessed an impressive paleontological collection, like all good and ambitious museums, it longed for a dinosaur to call its own.

Enter the Black Hills Institute of Geological Research, whose founder, Peter Larson, had discovered a quarry of Edmontosaurus *near Rapid City, South Dakota. The institute proposed that if Dr. Klaus W. Westphal, the museum's director, could put together a team to assist in the excavation of the duckbills, one complete skeleton could return to Madison with the diggers. Call it an import.*

It didn't take long for Westphal to assemble a team of expert and student geologists to assist Larson on his quarry excavation. The Wisconsin volunteers, along with a crew from the Black Hills institute, spent thousands of dollars in work-hours traveling to the dig, chiseling bone from stone, and transporting the goods during three consecutive summers, earning a full skeleton for study and display.

That Edmontosaurus *is exhibited at the Geology Museum today, along with dozens of other stand-out fossils they've collected through the years. Thanks to the Black Hills Institute of Geological Research, museums in non-dinosaur environments aren't shut out of the dinosaur adventure!*

Ice Age Interpretive Center
State Hwy. 35
PO Box 703
St. Croix Falls, WI 54024
(715) 483-3747
Web site: http://www.dnr.state.wi.us/org/land/parks/specific
    interstate
E-mail: Juliann.Fox@dnr.state.wi.us

MUSEUM OF NATURAL HISTORY

This great teaching museum offers an exhibit that's practically a geology education. Measuring geologic time, digging for evidence, Triassic fossils, Jurassic fossils, Cretaceous fossils—the whole spectrum is covered in a manner accessible to the general public, with great fossils and fossil images to support each important fact or point. Look for dozens of outstanding specimens, including a *Tyrannosaurus rex* skull, a duckbill femur, teeth, eggshell fragments, claws, vertebrae, and much, *much* more. It's a wonderful, little-known place to discover.

University of Wisconsin—Stevens Point
900 Reserve St.
Stevens Point, WI 54481
(715) 346-2858
Web site: http://www.uwsp.edu/museum
E-mail: emarks@uwsp.edu

Tyrannosaurus rex

**WISCONSIN GEOLOGICAL AND
NATURAL HISTORY SURVEY**
3817 MINERAL POINT RD.
MADISON, WI 53705
(608) 262-1705
WEB SITE: HTTP://WWW.UWEX.EDU/WGNHS
E-MAIL: BCBRISTOLL@WISC.EDU
(BILL C. BRISTOLL, INFORMATION MANAGER)

WYOMING

TATE GEOLOGICAL MUSEUM

Famed paleontologist Dr. Robert T. Bakker helped start this wonderful Wyoming museum in the late 1990s. Today, dozens of specimens collected by experts like director David Brown and students studying paleontology at the college are on display. *Monolophosaurus,* "Wyomingraptor," *Apatosaurus,* and *Tyrannosaurus rex,* along with marine reptiles and prehistoric mammals, are all exhibited. Volunteer dig opportunities are also possible, so be sure to check with the museum before you schedule your visit.

125 College Dr.

Casper, WY 82601

(307) 268-2447

Web site: http://www.cc.whecn.edu/tate/main.htm

E-mail: dbrown@caspercollege.edu (David Brown, director)

WYOMING STATE MUSEUM

Several exhibits at the Wyoming State Museum deal with the region's natural history. R.I.P.: Rex in Pieces is the exhibit with the most dinosaur appeal. Wyoming, according to the museum, is a dinosaur graveyard, with fossilized bones scattered across the landscape. Its fossil resources are so great, Wyoming played an important part in the turn-of-the-century Bone Wars between East Coast dinosaur hunters racing to discover new kinds of prehistoric beasts.

This particular exhibit features a *Camptosaurus* skeleton, because it was one of the first species found in Wyoming.

Barrett Bldg.
2301 Central Ave.
Cheyenne, WY 82002
(307) 777-7022
Web site: http://wyomuseum.state.wy.us
E-mail: wsm@state.wy.us

THE GREYBULL MUSEUM

Because Wyoming is so rich in fossil resources, most local history museums can feature geology. The dinosaur bones exhibited at the Greybull Museum were excavated only a short distance from the museum itself. Not an extensive collection, but worth seeing.

325 Greybull Ave.
PO Box 348
Greybull, WY 82426
(307) 765-2444
Web site: http://www.wyshs.org/mus-greybull.htm
E-mail: NA

FOSSIL BUTTE NATIONAL MONUMENT

Individual animals are frequently fossilized and offer a limited glimpse into the world in which they once lived. But at Fossil Butte National Monument, a 50-million-year-old lake bed captured the fossilized evidence of an entire ecosystem, including plants, insects, fish, reptiles, birds, and mammals! Kids five to fifteen can study and help prepare a prehistoric fossil as part of the National Park Service's Junior Ranger program when they visit this park.

PO Box 592
Kemmerer, WY 83101
(307) 877-4455
Web site: http://www.nps.gov/fobu
E-mail: form on Web site

Camptosaurus

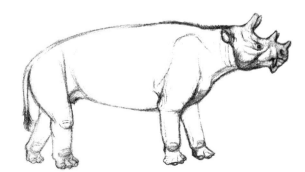

UNIVERSITY OF WYOMING GEOLOGICAL MUSEUM

Devoted to both education and public enlightenment, this teaching museum offers a great cross section of Wyoming's rich geologic history. One of its most fascinating specimens is "Big Al"—a young *Allosaurus,* discovered by the Bureau of Land Management in 1991, near Shell in northern Wyoming. A 25-foot cast, or exact copy, of its skeleton is on display, along with thousands of other paleontological and geological exhibits.

BONE DIGGER BONUS

FOSSIL BUTTE FOSSIL RANGERS

by Rachael Benton
Staff Paleontologist, Fossil Butte National Monument

When you think of park rangers, you think of someone with a shiny badge who answers questions—someone on a first-name basis with Smokey the Bear. All that's true. But now there is a special breed of ranger who not only takes care of trees and wildlife but also watches over fossils. I suppose you could call them "fossil rangers."

That's what I am—a ranger who takes care of fossils.

Did you know that many of our national parks contain important fossils? Because they are within the National Park system, they belong to all of the citizens of the United States of America.

Fossils are important resources that give us information about what Earth used to be like millions of years ago. They can tell us about climates and about how plants and animals have changed. But just like wildlife, fossils need to be protected. If we allow fossils to be stolen or to erode away, we lose important information about Earth's history. How do we protect fossils on federal lands? Mostly we start with the kids who visit the parks. We try to show them how important fossils are and explain why fossils need to be protected.

There are lots of things that kids can do at fossil parks. Many parks have lots of neat fossil exhibits, and sometimes there are people preparing fossils in a nearby lab. Park rangers also offer special programs on how to identify types of fossils. Some rangers show kids how to make casts, or copies, of fossils.

Rangers also protect fossils by encouraging scientists to visit the parks and study the fossils found there. If fossils are not collected and studied, they will soon erode away and turn to dust.

Finally, it is illegal to collect fossils on federal land without special permission, so rangers keep a watchful eye over the fossils. I hope you will take the time on your travels to stop and visit a fossil park.

S. H. Knight Geology Bldg.
University of Wyoming
1000 E. University Ave.
Laramie, WY 80271
(307) 766-2646
Web site: http://www.uwyo.edu/geomuseum
E-mail: geoms@uwyo.edu

BIGHORN CANYON VISITORS CENTER

Though there are a few dinosaur fossils exhibited in the visitors center, the primary focus of the geology exhibits on-site are primarily focused on ancient mammals. One of the best aspects of this stop, however, is the interpretive hiking trail that leads to a bone bed left behind by prehistoric creatures. A wild horse sanctuary is not far from this prehistoric location.

20 Hwy. 14A E.
Lovell, WY 82431
(307) 548-2251
Web site: http://www.nps.gov/bica
E-mail: form on Web site

SHERIDAN COLLEGE GEOLOGY MUSEUM

Since 1989, the Sheridan College Geology Department has been working the nearby Sheridan College dinosaur quarry by permission of the U.S. government. A number of Jurassic dinosaur specimens have been unearthed, including *Allosaurus, Torvosaurus, Camarasaurus, Diplodocus, Apatosaurus, Stegosaurus,* crocodiles, and much more. Many of the fossils are exhibited at the college geology museum.

3059 Coffeen Ave.
Sheridan, WY 82801
(800) 913-9139
(307) 674-6446
Web site: http://www.sheridan.edu/
   discover/museum.htm
E-mail: mflynn@sheridan.edu

Torvosaurus

182

WYOMING DINOSAUR CENTER

Thermopolis was a quiet little town before dinosaurs were discovered there. Cattle roamed the countryside. Children played baseball. Families shared picnics at the park. They still do all those things, the cows and kids and families. But now, there's a dinosaur museum in town. The Wyoming Dinosaur Center brought prehistoric life back to the future in 1995 with nineteen life-size models and skeletal replicas, as well as authentic fossils unearthed on-site. It also offers regular summer dinosaur digs for people of all ages. Expect to see *Allosaurus, Apatosaurus, Camarasaurus, Diplodocus, Triceratops,* and *T. rex,* along with ancient sea creatures and much more. This is one of my favorite dinosaur stops of all time—an all-purpose experience for dinosaur fans of all ages.

110 Carter Ranch Rd.

PO Box 868

Thermopolis, WY 82443

(800) 455-3466

(307) 864-2997

Web site: http://www.wyodino.org

E-mail: wdinoc@wyodino.org

WYOMING STATE GEOLOGICAL SURVEY
PO BOX 1347
LARAMIE, WY 82073
(307) 766-2286
WEB SITE: HTTP://WWW.WSGSWEB.UWYO.EDU
E-MAIL: WSGS-INFO@UWYO.EDU

Triceratops

Yukon Territory

Great Bear Lake

Northwest Territories

Great Slave Lake

Lake Athabasca

British Columbia

Alberta

Saskatchewan

Manitoba

Newfoundland

Lake Winnipeg

Quebec

Ontario

P.E.I.

New Brunswick

Lake Superior

Nova Scotia

Lake Huron

Lake Ontario

Lake Michigan

Lake Erie

ALBERTA

CALGARY ZOO PREHISTORIC PARK

Visiting Calgary's Prehistoric Park is a little like going back in time to the Age of Dinosaurs. Every effort has been made to create the look it might have had during that prehistoric time. More than one hundred species of plants and a virtual *herd* of life-size dinosaur models complete the ancient environment that gave the dinosaurs a reign of more than 180 million years—thirty-six times as long as man's time on Earth, so far.

1300 Zoo Rd. NE
Calgary, Alberta
Canada T2E 7V6
(800) 588-9993
Web site: http://www.calgaryzoo.org
E-mail: piercea@calgaryzoo.ab.ca (Webmaster)

FRANK SLIDE INTERPRETIVE CENTRE

In April 1903, half of the sleepy town of Frank was suddenly swallowed up by 82 million tons of limestone that crashed down from the summit of Turtle Mountain. About 70 of the town's 600 citizens were killed in the geologic disaster. And layers of geologic history were revealed in the limestone that cost them their lives. Today, through exhibits, videos, and guided tours, the Frank Slide Interpretive Centre takes a closer look at the shocking disaster and the fossil evidence it left behind.

PO Box 959, Blairmore
Crowsnest Pass, Alberta
Canada T0K 0E0
(403) 562-7388
Web site: http://www.frankslide.com
E-mail: info@frankslide.com

Corythosaurus

DRUMHELLER VALLEY INTERPRETIVE CENTRE

Originally called the Drumheller Dinosaur and Fossil Museum, L. A. Duncan's collection of fossils and other Alberta artifacts is on display in this lovely mid-size museum and interpretive center. Expect marine reptiles, dinosaurs, petrified wood, coal, and other Red Deer River Valley treasures—including a great gift shop where you can buy common Alberta fossils (summer hours only).

> 335 First St. E.
> PO Box 2135
> Drumheller, Alberta
> Canada T0J 0Y0
> (403) 823-2593
> Web site: http://www.virtuallydrumheller.com/tour/interp.htm
> E-mail: form on Web site

BONE DIGGER BONUS

DRUMHELLER, DINOSAUR CAPITAL OF THE WORLD

The Drumheller Chamber of Commerce is proud of its paleo-resources and heralds their appeal and reach on a terrific Web site dedicated to those fossil treasures and the businesses that benefit from them. Be sure to check out the Web site for tips on exploring the Dinosaur Trail—a historic tour of dinosaur country hiked by nearly every famous bone hunter in paleo-history. See for yourself at http://www.dinosaurvalley.com.

ROYAL TYRRELL MUSEUM

If you've seen a dinosaur documentary on television, chances are you've seen Canadian dinosaur hunter Dr. Phil Currie. And if you've seen Dr. Currie, you've heard of the remarkable Royal Tyrrell Museum—one of the crown jewels of paleontology museums in North America. So many species of dinosaurs and other prehistoric animals are on display—in so many creative ways—it's tough to describe it all in a short passage. But expect to see *Albertosaurus, Centrosaurus, Coelophysis, Corythosaurus, Dromaeosaurus, Hadrosaurus, Hypacrosaurus, Lambeosaurus, Ornitholestes, Saurornitholestes, Tyrannosaurus,* and more. This is one of the top five dinosaur museums in the world.

Hwy. 838
Midland Provincial Park
Drumheller, Alberta
Canada T0J 0Y0
(888) 440-4240
Web site: http://www.tyrrellmuseum.com
E-mail: tyrrell.info@gov.ab.ca

DINOSAUR COUNTRY SCIENCE CAMP

Operated by the Drumheller Regional Science Council, this not-for-profit camp offers kids the chance to explore the natural world, past and present, in the badlands of Alberta. Finding fossils through prospecting and excavation is a big part of the camp experience. Paleontologist Robin Digby is the camp director and a certified teacher. Half-day and longer programs are available for kids and families.

PO Box 516
East Coulee, Alberta
Canada T0J 1B0
(403) 822-3976
Web site: http://www.telusplanet.net/public/groundwk/index.html
E-mail: dinocamp@telusplanet.net

THE ROYAL ALBERTA MUSEUM

Quaternary paleontology is the study of fossil organisms that lived during the last 1.8 million years in the Pleistocene Epoch—the Ice Age—or within the Holocene, during the last 10,000 years. The Quaternary paleontology section of this Canadian museum includes hundreds of prehistoric specimens from that special class of fossils.

Geology Program
12845 102nd Ave.
Edmonton, Alberta
Canada T5N 0M6
(780) 453-9100
Web site: http://www.royalalbertamuseum.ca
E-mail: PMA.Webeditor@gov.ab.ca

UNIVERSITY OF ALBERTA PALEONTOLOGY MUSEUM

From the Web site: "The paleontology collections are an excellent way to journey back in time to an astounding and diverse ancient world. With over 2 million invertebrate fossils, the collections are a comprehensive record of dynamic, early invertebrate life. A great number of the specimens are unique, collected in the 1950s and 1960s by petroleum companies during oil exploration in western and northern Canada and donated to the University of Alberta in the 1970s. Combined with fossils collected elsewhere in the world, the specimens are a valuable and engaging resource for students, researchers, and the public." Some of the best specimens are displayed in this top-notch paleontology museum.

B-01 Earth Sciences Bldg.

11223 Saskatchewan Dr.

Edmonton, Alberta

Canada T6G 2E1

(780) 492-3265

Web site: http://www.museums.ualberta.ca

E-mail: form on Web site

DINOSAUR PROVINCIAL PARK—WORLD HERITAGE SITE

Stop in at the Tyrrell's field station in the heart of Dinosaur Provincial Park, 28 square miles of the richest fossil deposits in the world. A 7,000-square-foot visitors center with exhibits is in place at the field station, along with a fossil prep lab and a great bookstore. It was named a United Nations World Heritage Site in 1979 for its devotion to protecting the world's natural resources.

PO Box 50

Patricia, Alberta

Canada T0J 2K0

(403) 378-4342

Web site: http://www.cd.gov.ab.ca/parks/dinosaur

E-mail: form on Web site

Ceratosaurus

COURTENAY AND DISTRICT MUSEUM OF PALEONTOLOGY CENTRE

An elasmosaur found in the Puntledge River leads off the paleontology tour at this great British Columbia museum. Other vertebrate fossils, including mosasaurs, turtles, and fish—along with invertebrate fossils—round out the collection to make it a terrific experience for families searching for ancient marine fossils near the U.S.–Canadian border on the West Coast. Want to collect a few 80-million-year-old fossils you can keep? Take the museum's official fossil tour. After a ten-minute drive and a five-minute hike, you can gather common marine fossils for your collection under the supervision of museum staffers. Find something rare or scientifically important, and you'll have to donate it to the museum. But the finder's name will be credited with the discovery on museum records.

207 Fourth St.
Courtenay, British Columbia
Canada V9N 1G7
(250) 334-0686
Web site: http://www.courtenaymuseum.ca
E-mail: museum@island.net

THE YOHO-BURGESS SHALE FOUNDATION

This educational and rustic fossil hiking program named for the famous rock formation is top-notch as it stands—a great way to learn about British Columbia's geologic past. But a proposed Burgess Shale Earth and Life Science Learning Centre may turn this into a one-of-a-kind hands-on educational facility for kids in upper elementary, middle, and high schools across North America.

PO Box 148
Field, British Columbia
Canada V0A 1G0
(800) 343-3006 (hike reservations)
(250) 343-6006
Web site: http://www.burgess-shale.bc.ca
E-mail: info@burgess-shale.bc.ca

THE EXPLORATION PLACE

Discover the fossils of northern British Columbia, both online and at this exciting museum in Prince George. The Web site explains, "Millions of years ago, British Columbia was covered by water. In the water lived the ancestors of today's plants and animals. Over millions of years, organisms lived, died, and evolved. Some of these plants and animals are preserved as fossils in the sedimentary rock of today." Here's a great way to expand your paleo-knowledge beyond U.S. borders.

The Fraser–Fort George Regional Museum
333 Becott Pl.
Prince George, British Columbia
Canada V2L 4V7
(250) 562-1612
Web site: http://www.theexplorationplace.com
E-mail: info@theexplorationplace.com

ROYAL BRITISH COLUMBIA MUSEUM

Fossils from the region are exhibited in the Natural History Gallery, as is a fleshed-out woolly mammoth that died in British Columbia about 13,000 years ago. This mammoth is the museum's unofficial symbol. Traveling exhibits with fossil themes are frequently offered.

675 Belleville St.
Victoria, British Columbia
Canada V8V 9W2
(888) 447-7977
(250) 356-7226
Web site: http://rbcm1.rbcm.gov.bc.ca
E-mail: reception@royalbcmuseum.bc.ca

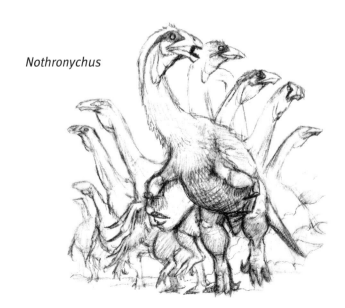

Nothronychus

191

MANITOBA

THE MANITOBA MUSEUM

This museum's geology collection is extensive and focuses on vertebrate and invertebrate fossils from Manitoba and other parts of the world. Fossil plants, insects, mollusks, and meteorites are also part of the exhibit.

190 Rupert Ave.
Winnipeg, Manitoba
Canada R3B 0N2
(204) 956-2830
Web site: http://www.manitobamuseum.ca/home.html
E-mail: info@manitobamuseum.ca

NOVA SCOTIA

NOVA SCOTIA MUSEUM OF NATURAL HISTORY

The Fossils of Nova Scotia is a terrific exhibit. Discoveries, famous scientists, fossil preservation, geologic history, even great dinosaur books are part of the museum's fossil outreach effort. Eight time frames—from Silurian to Quaternary—are examined, featuring dozens of animal specimens in fossil form. Fossil evidence of North America's oldest dinosaur (160 million years older than *Tyrannosaurus rex*) and the Bone Zone play area are just part of this museum's paleo-offerings.

1747 Summer St.
Halifax, Nova Scotia
Canada B3H 3A6
(902) 424-7353
Web site: http://www.museum.gov.ns.ca/mnh
E-mail: form on Web site

FUNDY GEOLOGICAL MUSEUM

Project Prosauropod may be the most important feature on this museum's Web site. Why? Because it helps us understand how important this very ancient dinosaur might be to the history of life on Earth and prehistoric dinosaurs. A full-size, 6-foot-long, fleshed-out dinosaur model and a skeletal replica of the 200-million-year-old species are both on display. But the exciting online (and offline) prosauropod research lab will give you a closer look at this very ancient dinosaur and the new evidence it reveals as paleontologists study its unusual fossils.

PO Box 640
Parrsboro, Nova Scotia
Canada B0M 1S0
(866) 856-3466
(902) 254-3814
Web site: http://www.museum.gov.ns.ca/fgm
E-mail: fundygeo@gov.ns.ca or dinoproj@gov.ns.ca

MILLER MUSEUM OF GEOLOGY

The Dawn of Life exhibit is a look at 3 billion years of life on Earth. But many other fossil topics are explored at this educational museum designed to be a school outreach resource. Dinosaurs, earthquakes, meteorites, and geology are some themes on display.

Department of Geological Sciences
Miller Hall
Queen's University
Kingston, Ontario
Canada K7L 3N6
(613) 533-6767
Web site: http://www.geol.queensu.ca/museum/museum.html
E-mail: badham@geol.queensu.ca

Plateosaurus

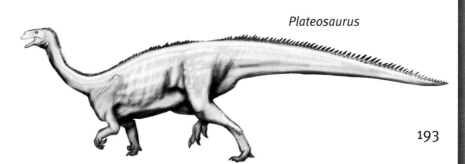

CANADIAN MUSEUM OF NATURE

The life-size, fleshed-out model of *Daspletosaurus torosus* (created by Research Casting International in Beamsville, Ontario) makes visiting this museum worth the trip. It's remarkable. But the whole Dinosaur Gallery is outstanding. You'll see *Chasmosaurus,* flying reptile *Pteranodon,* the coelacanth fish, a true "living fossil," and more.

240 McLeod St.

PO Box 3443, Station D

Ottawa, Ontario

Canada K1P 6P4

(800) 263-4433

(613) 566-4700

Web site: http://www.nature.ca

Daspletosaurus link: http://www.nature.ca/exhibits/atrium/
myst_e.cfm

E-mail: questions@mus-nature.ca

BRUCE COUNTY MUSEUM

According to the Web site, "DINO-MIGHT features seven full-size cast skeletons, four wall-mounted cast skeletons, six cast dinosaur skulls (including a *Tyrannosaurus rex* skull), a Dino-Dig sandbox, a 'walk-through' rib cage, several partially fleshed-out cast specimens, and much more!" Look for *Malawisaurus, Albertosaurus, Centrosaurus, Deinonychus, Coelophysis,* and a nest of eggs.

33 Victoria St. N.

PO Box 180

Southampton, Ontario

Canada N0H 2L0

(866) 318-8889

(519) 797-2080

Web site: http://www.brucecounty.on.ca/museum/dinosaurs/
dinosaurs.htm

E-mail: museum@brucecounty.on.ca

Coelophysis

194

ROYAL ONTARIO MUSEUM

Dozens of great exhibits are worth discovering at this museum, but Maiasaur Project: The Life and Times of a Dinosaur is one of the best prehistoric options in Ontario. Experts spent two years creating this tribute to the "good mother" dinosaur, complete with a life-size model, skeletons, a prep lab, and many other exhibits designed to better understand the life and death of this duck-billed dinosaur. It is the fifteenth dinosaur added to the ROM's collection. There's a lot more to see.

> 100 Queen's Park
> Toronto, Ontario
> Canada M5S 2C6
> (416) 586-8000
> Web site: http://www.rom.on.ca
> Maiasaur Project site: http://www.rom.on.ca/palaeo/maiasaur
> E-mail: form on Web site

REDPATH MUSEUM

Approximately 150,000 fossils are housed within this educational museum's paleontology collection. Many are on display, and they are regularly rotated. Imagine a rare sea snail from the Ordovician Period, 450 million years ago, or a mounted *Albertosaurus* skeleton. These and many other fossils from the region are on display.

> 859 Sherbrooke St. W.
> Montreal, Quebec
> Canada H3A 2K6
> (514) 398-4086
> Web site: http://www.redpath-museum.mcgill.ca
> Alternate Web site: http://www.mcgill.ca/redpath/
>   collections/paleontology
> E-mail: ad14@musica.lan.mcgill.ca

Albertosaurus

LAKE TIMISKAMING FOSSIL CENTRE

"The Earth Before the Dinosaurs" is the core theme of this fascinating museum of prehistoric fossils from the Ordovician and Silurian periods. It's a look at life in the earliest stages of evolution.

PO Box 296

Notre-Dame-du-Nord, Quebec

Canada J0Z 3B0

(819) 723-2500

Web site: http://www.rlcst.qc.ca/index2.html

E-mail: fossiles@sympatico.ca

SASKATCHEWAN

EASTEND'S DINOCOUNTRY

Even before the bone diggers of Saskatchewan discovered "Scotty"—a remarkable *T. rex*—in 1994, plans were in the works for the *T. rex* Discovery Centre in Eastend. The idea was to showcase the science and fantasy of the amazing meat-eater—and other fossil resources in the region—through exhibits, models, paleontological lab work, and film.

T. rex Discovery Centre

Box 646

Eastend, Saskatchewan

Canada S0N 0T0

(306) 295-4009

Web site: http://www.dinocountry.com

E-mail: t.rex1@sasktel.net

ROYAL SASKATCHEWAN MUSEUM

The Earth Science Gallery is well worth the trip to Regina. Along with dinosaurs, you'll find information about microfossils, type fossils, types of sediment and concretion, mammals, reptiles, rodents, and various fossil experts. For younger fossil fans, there is the Paleo Pit, a learning center with hands-on activities.

2445 Albert St.
Regina, Saskatchewan
Canada S4P 4W7
(306) 787-2815
Web site: http://www.royalsaskmuseum.ca
E-mail: rsminfo@royalsaskmuseum.ca

Therizinosaur baby

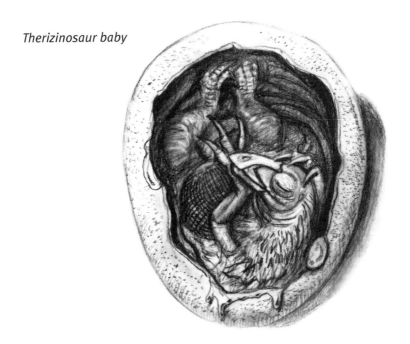

DINOSAUR SHOPPING GUIDE

DINO PRODUCTS

AMERICAN DINOSAUR FOSSIL EXCHANGE

Beautiful replicas of famous fossil slabs, skulls, and bones, as well as real fossils, are for sale, along with supplies for traveling dinosaur events and exhibits.

> 1 Penny Ln.
> Montebello, NY 10901
> (800) 411-3466
> (845) 368-3466
> Web site: http://www.americandinosaurfossilsexchange.com
> E-mail: info@americandinosaurfossilexchange.com

HANMAN'S FOSSIL REPLICAS AND MINERALS

A good selection of dinosaur, bird, fish, invertebrate, mammal, and reptile fossil replicas for almost every collector's budget can be found here.

> Andrew R. Milner
> PO Box 1616
> Parowan, UT 84761
> (435) 477-9467
> Web-site: http://www.hanmansfossils.com
> E-mail: andrew@hanmansfossils.com

PREHISTORIC PLANET STORE

WOW! It's tough to overstate the fossil replica materials available through this organization. As the Web site says, "We cast, resell, and broker essentially every museum-quality replica fossil available today, from tiny trilobites to enormous, full-size dinosaur skeletons." A wonderful resource for educators and fossil fans. Author's favorite: everything! How can you pick from such a dream-come-true selection? It's *all* amazing.

> PO Box 200
> Barrackville, WV 26559
> (800) 822-6788
> (304) 366-1810
> Web site: http://www.paleoclones.com
> E-mail: form on Web site

TWO GUYS FOSSILS

Craving a perfect copy of a genuine dinosaur claw, tooth, bone, or other fossilized body part? Want ammonites, crinoids, insects, trilobites, or amber samples? You may find it at Two Guys Fossils, along with other gift items, including models, posters, books, jewelry, household items—even checkbook covers and mouse pads! Author's favorite: the *Velociraptor*-claw pendant and the fossil-slab coffee table.

1 Lynnes Way

East Bridgewater, MA 02333

(800) FOSSILS (367-7457)

Web site: http://www.twoguysfossils.com

E-mail: app@twoguysfossils.com

OTHER DINO-RELATED PRODUCTS: ART PRINTS AND SCULPTURES

DAVID KRENTZ PRESENTZ

David Krentz has done commissioned work for film studios, including Disney, Sony, and Columbia, and for educational organizations like the California Institute for the Arts, the Society of Vertebrate Paleontology, and more. These are beautiful, accurate dinosaur art pieces you can paint yourself. His bronze models are very expensive, but the resin options are more affordable in many instances.

250 Redwood Dr.

Pasadena, CA 91105

Web site: http://www.krentzpresentz.com

E-mail: david@krentzpresentz.com

THE DINOSAUR STUDIO, INC.

Dan LoRusso is a professional dinosaur sculptor whose work is featured in museums all over the country. But he also sculpts for the general public. These are *very* expensive art pieces for serious collectors only. Lovely work from one of the best.

98 Yeomans Ave.

Medford, MA 02155

(781) 396-8066

Web site: http://www.dinosaurstudio.com
E-mail: webmaster@dinosaurstudio.com

DINOTOPIA STORE

If you love James Gurney's magical world called Dinotopia, you'll love the chance to buy the books, art prints, notecards, and other collectibles from his Web site—many of which are personally autographed.

PO Box 693

Rhinebeck, NY 12572

Web site: http://www.dinotopia.com

E-mail: webmaster@dinotopia.com

HEALTHSTONES DINOSTORE

High-quality dinosaur art reproductions, models, plaques, magnets, and key chains can be bought at this online store.

(818) 348-8726

Web site: http://www.healthstones.com

E-mail: comments@healthstones.com

PALEOCRAFT RESIN MODEL KITS

You'll find not just dinosaurs but prehistoric mammal models crafted of resin to build and paint on your own. A terrific, sometimes unusual selection.

c/o Area 53

26067 E. 760 Rd.

Wagoner, OK 74467

Web site: http://www.paleocraft.com

E-mail: area53@paleocraft.com

SKULLDUGGERY, INC.

This is one of the first successful fossil-replica companies.

624 S. B St.

Tustin, CA 92780

(714) 832-8488

Web site: http://www.skullduggery.com

E-mail: form on Web site

CLOTHING

ABSOLUTE TIES AND SOCKS ONLINE

You'll find a great assortment of dinosaur socks and ties for all ages.

54 Great Hill Rd.
Naugatuck, CT 06770
(877) 532-6588
Web site: http://www.absoluteties.com/dinosaurs.html
E-mail: absolties@aol.com

DINOSOLES

Every dinosaur fan will want to stomp *large* in these exceptional sneakers made by Dinosoles. But only small feet will get so lucky. These shoes—featuring 3-D dinosaurs, dinosaur eyes, and dinosaur track-makers built into the soles—are, technically, for kids only. But if you're like me and managed to keep relatively small feet into adulthood, you might be able to squeeze into a pair and share in the fun. They are comfy, classy, well constructed, and completely cool. Check out the Web site today!

9256 Deering Ave.
Chatsworth, CA 91311
(818) 721-1404
Web site: http://www.dinosoles.com
E-mail: info@dinosoles.com

THE SCIENCE TEECHER

Great dinosaur T-shirts, as well as other math- and science-themed items, are for sale.

196 N. Saratoga
St. Paul, MN 55104
(877) 286-6212
Web site: http://www.scienceteecher.com/dinosaurs.htm
E-mail: scienceteecher@usfamily.net

Titanis

EDUCATIONAL

ALLPOSTERS.COM

A great selection of dinosaur posters is available for online perusing.

2100 Powell St., 13th Fl.

Emeryville, CA 94608

(888) 654-0143

Web site: http://www.animal-posters.net/dinosaur-dinosaurs.html

E-mail: orders@allposters.com

DINOSAUR DISCOVERY

Teachers with a dinosaur tilt will love the creative options offered by Dinosaur Discovery, including dinosaur reconstruction kits, curriculum and activity guides, dinosaur dig simulations, and more. The Web site even offers slide-show presentations of classrooms using their materials so you can see how other teachers have applied the goods. This is a terrific resource.

65 N. Shore Rd.

Newport, NH 03773

(603) 863-0066

Web site: http://www.dinosaurdiscovery.com

E-mail: info@dinosaurdiscovery.com

WALLS OF THE WILD

Here you'll find absolutely amazing animal stickers for use on bedroom, classroom, or exhibit walls—dinosaurs, including *T. rex, Stegosaurus,* and *Triceratops,* as well as other exotic animals and related accessories (like palm trees and coral reefs). Astonishing—don't miss these!

19 Palmyra Rd.

Brewster, NY 10509

(845) 278-4612

Web site: http://www.wallsofthewild.com

E-mail: zoo@wallsofthewild.com

Lesothosaurus

FIGURES

LINK AND PIN HOBBIES

This site has a great selection of dinosaur figures.

> 5508 Irish Spring St.
> Las Vegas, NV 89149
> (702) 839-1733
> Web site: http://www.linkandpinhobbies.com
> E-mail: nanorex@ix.netcom.com

SAFARI, LTD.

For years, museums and quality toy stores have carried the Safari Carnegie Museum of Natural History line of dinosaur replica figures—individual, to-scale, hand-painted models. They are some of the best dinosaur figures available in the world.

> 1400 NW 159th St., Ste. 104
> Miami Gardens, FL 33169
> (800) 554-5414
> (305) 621-1000
> Web site: http://www.safariltd.com
> E-mail: form on Web site

FOOD

A CANDY FIX

Send a Dinosaur Candy Gram—a bucketful of sweet dinosaur treats.

> 8138 Roaring Springs Rd.
> Gloucester, VA 23061
> (804) 695-9310
> Web site: http://www.acandyfix.safeshopper.com/15/263.htm?712
> E-mail: acandyfix@aol.com

CANDYWAREHOUSE

Great selection of dino-themed threats, including Dinosaur Candy Climbers—little dinosaurs that cling to stick candy as they "climb" to delicious heights.

> 5314 Third St.
> Irwindale, CA 91706
> (626) 480-0899
> Web site: http://www.candywarehouse.com
> E-mail: sales@candywarehouse.com

PARTYPALOOZA

Partypalooza sells prepackaged "goodie bags" for children's dinosaur parties—in three sizes.

> 641 Harper Dr.
> Glassboro, NJ 08028
> (888) 397-2328
> (856) 881-7676
> Web site: http://www.partypalooza.com/DinosaursCU.html
> E-mail: form on Web site

SUGARCRAFT

The Dino-Mighty Kit is a really creative dino-habitat cake-and-candy set.

> 2715 Dixie Hwy.
> Hamilton, OH 45015
> (513) 896-7089
> Web site: http://www.sugarcraft.com/dino.htm
> E-mail: form on Web site

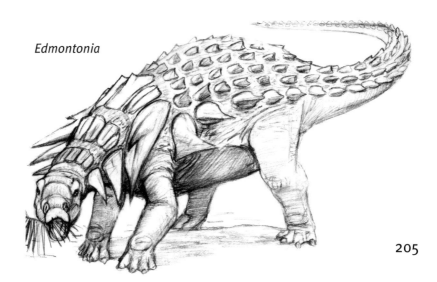

Edmontonia

GAMES

STEVE JACKSON GAMES

Dino Hunt is a complicated, but educational, family board game for players ages eight and up. Dino Hunt explores different eras in which dinosaurs thrived through competition. Gather dinosaurs, keep them healthy, and win the game!

(866) 366-7323

Web site: http://www.sjgames.com/dinohunt

E-mail: orders@warehouse23.com

JEWELRY

BERNARDINE FINE ART JEWELRY

These are specially designed men's and women's jewelry items made with polished dinosaur-bone pieces—very expensive.

4333 Homer Ave.

Cincinnati, OH 45227

(888) 675-0689

(513) 561-3057

Web site: http://www.bernardine.com/dinosaurbone-jewelry.htm

E-mail: bernardine2@bernardine.com

BLUEMUD.COM

You'll find sterling-silver dinosaur and other prehistoric animal charms at very reasonable prices. E-mail for details.

17837 First Ave. S.

#513

Seattle, WA 98148

Web site: http://www.bluemud.com

E-mail: sales@bluemud.com

GOLDEN WONDERS

Lovely dinosaur charms, pins, pendants, and earrings from $30 to $500 are for sale at this online store.

4419 Valley Forge Rd.

Durham, NC 27705

(919) 382-0164

Web site: http://www.goldenwonders.com/

catalog.php?page=dino

E-mail: Info@goldenwonders.com

HEIRLOOM DESIGNER JEWELRY BY JAN McCLELLAN

Jewelry designed with dinosaur-bone pieces, amber, ammonite, and other mineral products are featured.

4939 Sumac Ct.

Klamath Falls, OR 97603

(800) 851-6052

(541) 884-6052

Web site: http://www.designjewel.com/dino_cab.htm

E-mail: jan@designjewel.com

MOAB BRUSHY BASIN JURASSIC GIFT FOSSILS

You'll find a fascinating selection of fossil-specific jewelry and gifts made of or enhanced by dinosaur bone, petrified wood, and other fossil treasures. Also available are polished samples of dinosaur bone and petrified wood.

PO Box 1416

Moab, UT 84532

Web site: http://www.brushybasin.com/body

_index.html

E-mail: support@brushybasin.com

PARK CITY JEWELERS

Featured is a series of rings with inlaid dinosaur bone—very expensive.

PO Box 3532

430 Main St.

Park City, UT 84060

(888) 340-5020

(435) 649-6550

Web site: http://www.parkcityjewelers.com/dinosaur

_bone_jewelry.asp

E-mail: info@parkcityjewelers.com

STEWART'S PETRIFIED WOOD TRADING POST

Various jewelry items with polished slices of petrified wood, as well as petrified wood samples, are for sale.

PO Box 68

Holbrook, AZ 86025

(On I-40 east of Holbrook)

(800) 414-8533

Web site: http://www.petrifiedwood.com

E-mail: cstewa24@frontiernet.net

MULTIPLE DINOSAUR ITEMS

ACADEMY OF NATURAL SCIENCES

This store offers stuffed animals, cups, puzzles, 3-D kits, models, toys, sweatshirts, and books. Author's favorite: blue ceramic latte mug with a great *Triceratops* logo.

Museum Shop Online

1900 Benjamin Franklin Pkwy.

Philadelphia, PA 19103

(215) 299-1186

Web site: http://www.acnatsci.org/shop

E-mail: shop@acnatsci.org

ANIMAL DEN

Here you'll find address labels, mouse pads, puppets, T-shirts, calendars, and plush animals. Author's favorite: the dinosaur mouse pad.

2459 SE T.V. Hwy.

#461

Hillsboro, OR 97123

(503) 844-6136

Web site: http://www.animalden.com/dinosaur.html

E-mail: ar@animalden.com

THE DINOSAUR FARM

The Dinosaur Farm features wall clings, sleeping bags, figures, lamps, door hangers, wallpaper borders, sheets, books, lunchboxes, masks, skeleton kits, throw quilts, party materials, and more. Author's favorite: wall cling . . . it's big and it's bad (a meat-eating *Herrerasaurus*)—too cool for words!

1510 Mission St.

South Pasadena, CA 91030

(888) 658-2388

(626) 441-2767

Web site: http://www.dinosaurfarm.com

E-mail: info@dinofarm.com

DINOSAUR NEST

The Dinosaur Nest has figures, wooden puzzles, bouncy balls, stuffed animals, and dig kits. Author's favorite: the *Velociraptor* 3-D wooden puzzle kit (it's large . . . and I mean *large!*).

PO Box 501

Stephenville, TX 76401

Web site: http://www.thedinosaurnest.com

E-mail: help@storeforknowledge.com

DINOSAUR SHOP AT THE ABOYD COMPANY

Toys, games, models, statues, books, music, posters, videos, masks, and arts and crafts are some of the featured items. Author's favorite: Skull Skill reconstruction kits—*Tyrannosaurus rex*. An amazing project for older kids and adults.

PO Box 4568

Jackson, MS 39296

(888) 458-2693

Web site: http://www.aboyd.com

E-mail: info@aboyd.com

DINOSAUR STUFF

Featured are puppets, games, replicas, clothing, novelties, inflatables, and balloons. Author's favorite: the dinosaur chess set is pretty amazing, but I also love the Raptor Jacks—a traditional game of jacks where you pick up raptors instead of jacks as you bounce the ball (included).

Kissimmee, FL 34741

(800) 842-9613

Web site: http://www.dinosaurstuff.com

E-mail: info@alltherightstuff.com

DINOSAUR SUPERSTORE

You'll find toys, science activities, replicas, plush animals, T-shirts, room decor, games, puzzles, and birthday party supplies. Author's favorite: birthday supplies (a great selection).

(888) 446-8838

Web site: http://www.dinosaursuperstore.com

E-mail: gina@dinosaursuperstore.com

DINOSAUR WORLD

Everything dinosaur you could dream of to buy or examine (well, almost everything) is at this store.

4242 Medical Dr., Ste. 1200

San Antonio, TX 78229

(210) 798-6224

Web site: http://www.dinosaurworld.com

E-mail: form on Web site

FOREVER IN SEASON

Quilts, place mats, pillow shams, bath towels, tote bags, table runners, etc. Search for *dinosaurs* on the Web site.

PO Box 294581

Lewisville, TX 75029

(866) 784-5776

(972) 446-8234

Web site: http://www.foreverinseason.com

E-mail: info@foreverinseason.com

KRITTERS IN THE MAILBOX

This mail-order and online company offers a whole list of dinosaur items, including stuffed animals, cookie cutters, figurines, puzzles, puppets, signs, switch plates, and T-shirts. Author's favorite: *T. rex* crossing sign. They also offer six free e-mail postcards to send.

PO Box 271418

Flower Mound, TX 75027

Web site: http://www.krittersinthemailbox.com/animals/dinosaur

E-mail: sales@krittersinthemailbox.com

PREHISTORIC WORLD IMAGES

Featured are dinosaur calendars, T-shirts, sweatshirts, screen savers, posters, games, pictures, hats, toys, books, plush animals, puzzles, party toys, notecards, neckties, and art prints designed by Josef Moravec. (For more about Moravec, checkout this Web site.)

Online Dinosaur Store

631 N. Stephanie St., Ste. 431

Henderson, NV 89014

Web site: http://www.shop.store.yahoo.com/prehistory

E-mail: dinostore@prehistory.com

WORLD HERITAGE SHOPS

You'll find amazing dinosaur shopping choices at this British online store featuring books, fossil casts, jewelry, models, stuffed animals, games, stationery, and more. Click on the "Dinosaur Museum" link from the Glossary page.

Dinosaur Museum

25 High West St.

Dorchester

DT1 1UW

United Kingdom

44 (0) 1305 269741

Web site: http://www.whshop.co.uk

E-mail: info@whshop.co.uk

Therizinosaur rookery

PLUSH ANIMALS

BEANOSAURS BY PEPONI

There are many quality "beanie" stuffed dinosaurs modeled after different species. The Web site includes dinosaur facts about each one. *Very* cute option for dinosaur lovers young and old alike. Also available, a Beanosaurs collector's book with photos and details on each animal. Author's favorite: *Kentrosaurus*—pink with gray plates.

> Peponi International
> PO Box 1260
> Lake Havasu City, AZ 86405
> (800) 314-4750
> Web site: http://www.peponiplush.com/beanosaurs
> E-mail: customerservice@peponiplush.com

PUFFKINS COLLECTIBLES

SWIBCO's Puffkins line features at least four dinosaur characters—Danny, Dinky, Drake, and Pickles. You can order them through Cuddly Collectibles.

> Web site: http://www.cuddlycollectibles.com
> E-mail: whosit10@aol.com

SOAP AND BATH

EARTH REFLECTIONS DINO SOAP

Custom-made dinosaur soap—*Stegosaurus* or *Tyrannosaurus rex*—with your choice of color and scent is the featured dino-themed item.

> 3773 Sand Hill Circle
> South Jordan, UT 84095
> Web site: http://www.artsandcraftsfair.com/merchants/Earth
> E-mail: form on Web site

NOVELTY SOAP COMPANY

Check out the dinosaur-egg soap, among other dino-themed items.

> PO Box 20856
> Milwaukee, WI 53220

Web site: http://www.noveltysoapcompany.com
E-mail: customerservice@noveltysoapcompany.com

THE PONTE VEDRA SOAP SHOPPE
You'll find an assortment of dinosaur soap molds (four per box).

1520 Sawgrass Village Dr.

#212

Ponte Vedra Beach, FL 32082

(904) 543-8296

Web site: http://www.pvsoap.com/mold_dinos.asp

E-mail: contact@pvsoap.com

SPECIALTY ITEMS

ALLHEART.COM
Here you'll find professional medical supplies, including a dinosaur stethoscope cover and a dinosaur ZooPals pediatric exam table. Search for *dinosaurs* on the Web site.

431 Calle San Pablo

Camarillo, CA 93012

(805) 445-8816 (fax)

Web site: http://www.allheart.com

E-mail: customerservice@allheart.com

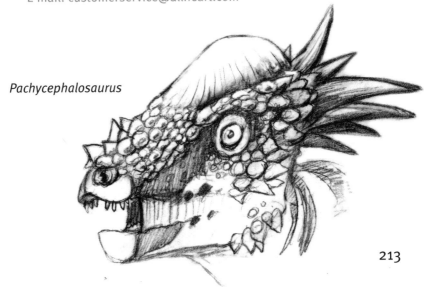

Pachycephalosaurus

Allosaurus

Stegosaurus

DINOSAUR LINKS

GENERAL DINOSAUR INFO

DINOBASE

This database, maintained by the University of Bristol in the United Kingdom, contains a great wealth of searchable information, including dinosaur species lists, dinosaur extinction theories, paleo-artist John Sibbick's artwork, and research specific to the University of Bristol.

http://www.palaeo.gly.bris.ac.uk/dinobase/dinopage.html

DINODATA

Fred Bervoets, who oversees this extensive group of dinosaur links, articles, and databases, insists his is not the most science-specific site on the Net. But Bervoets is being modest. The site includes content from exceptionally knowledgeable dinosaur enthusiasts like George Olshevsky and Mickey Mortimer. This is a site advanced paleontology fans could search for hours and hours without getting bored.

http://www.dinodata.net

DINO RUSS'S LAIR

Russ Jacobson is a name well known in paleontology circles, in part due to his Web site—one of the oldest paleo-resources on the Net. But he is, in his own right, a gifted student of paleontology, associated with many working scientists and projects in Colorado, Utah, Montana, and beyond. Look for books, pictures, articles, discussion boards, and much more on this classic site.

http://www.dinoruss.org

DINOSAURIA

Like Dino Russ, Jeff Poling has been chronicling dinosaur progress on the Internet for a long time, so his database is extensive. What he doesn't know, he'll find out. But after so many years of dedicated study, there can't be much he doesn't know! A great place for online dinosaur exploration from one of the original cyber-pioneers.

http://www.dinosauria.com

DINOSAURICON

T. Mike Keesey mans Dinosauricon, another extensive dino-source chock-full of dinosaur history, identification guides, article databases, and more. But the art and artist index is one of Keesey's most impressive Web site treasuries. A truly breathtaking collection of more than a thousand drawings, sculptures, paintings, and scientific sketches, and details on the artists who created them.

> http://www.dino.lm.com

DINOWEB

Teenager Alastair Reece is no professional dinosaur paleontologist, but he is devoted to dinosaurs and that passion shows in his DinoWeb list of paleontological theories, museum links, games, and much more.

> http://www.dino-web.com/index.html

DISCOVERY CHANNEL DINO GUIDE

If you've ever watched a dinosaur documentary on TV, chances are good you saw it on the Discovery Channel. The Dino Guide element of the Discovery Channel's overall Web presence offers a look at their popular Walking with Dinosaurs and Dinosaur Planet series, special dinosaur programming notes, and a brief look at dinosaur favorites through its database of images and factoids.

> http://www.dsc.discovery.com/guides/dinosaur/dinosaur.html

JURASSIC PARK INSTITUTE

One of the most professional and visually pleasing dinosaur worlds on the Net, this site offers "dinotainment," news, an encyclopedia of species, travel-stop factoids, teacher resource guides, and much more. It's user-friendly and features some contributions from noted paleontologists, including Neal Larson and Robert Bakker.

> http://www.jpinstitute.com

MAMA'S MINERALS FOSSIL LINKS

This is a commercial site that offers minerals and fossils for sale. But be sure to check out Mama's "Rock Hard Facts" index for a mini-education on fossils and other geological wonders.

> http://www.mamasminerals.com

SVP'S PALEONTOLOGY PORTAL

The SVP—Society of Vertebrate Paleontology—is the best-known professional organization of fossil experts in the United States, and perhaps the world. Its resources are vast, and its Internet clearinghouse, launched in May of 2005, offers fossil fans the chance to read about opportunities in specific regions and to post accurate facts of their own. Look for a fossil gallery, a resource bank, a calendar of paleontological events, and much more. At last, a central zone for all things prehistoric—with accuracy to spare!

http://www.paleoportal.org

WALKING WITH DINOSAURS

Based on one of the most popular dinosaur documentaries ever created, this user-friendly Web site offers short samples of the lifelike animation that made the *Walking with Dinosaurs* program so popular, as well as fact files, news briefs, a timeline, games, quizzes, and much, *much* more. A great resource for families and schools.

http://www.bbc.co.uk/dinosaurs

DINO ART

JOHN BINDON

Artist John Bindon has worked as a consultant and contributor for dinosaur documentaries, including *Beyond T. rex, Baby Dinosaurs,* and *When Dinosaurs Roamed America,* as well as the Disney feature film *Dinosaur.* His paintings are in museums across the country. And you can see many of his paintings on his Web site.

http://www.bindonart.com/dino.htm

FRANK DENOTA

DeNota's artwork is displayed by dinosaur type on this artist's easy-to-navigate Web site. Included are *Triceratops, Velociraptor, Amargasaurus, Tyrannosaurus,* and others.

http://frankdenota.blackhydra.com

Stegoceras

JOHN GURCHE

John Gurche is one of the most astonishing dinosaur illustrators ever to bring the prehistoric to life. His work has appeared on the cover of *National Geographic,* on U.S. postage stamps, and in museums and galleries around the world. He is an exceptional talent, and his Web site offers a look at his brilliance. Not to be missed.

http://www.gurche.com

DOUG HENDERSON

Doug Henderson is another of the greats in the realm of dinosaur artwork. His engaging Web site offers plenty of artistic samples (including dinosaurs in crayon and pencil from his early childhood) along with advice for up-and-coming artists with dinosaur dreams of their own. It's a warm, encouraging chance to look inside the life and development of a paleo-artist at the top of his game.

http://gallery.in-tch.com/~earthhistory

TODD MARSHALL

Todd Marshall has illustrated a number of dinosaur books for young readers, including the *Atlas of Dinosaurs,* along with articles, Web sites, and other professional dino-rich publications and visual projects. Like Doug Henderson's, his Web site explores how he got his start and why he loves the work he does, along with offering a great cross section of his work.

http://www.marshalls-art.com

LUIS V. REY'S ART GALLERY

Luis Rey (whose artwork graces this book) is a maverick in dinosaur artistry. His dinosaurs are much more than paintings. They are illustrations of dinosaur theory—pictures of dinosaur life reborn. His prehistoric creatures seem so real, they could climb off the page! This Web site captures Rey's energy and dedication to paleontological study. A real treat to explore.

http://www.luisrey.ndtilda.co.uk

JOHN SIBBICK

Though he also paints, Sibbick is popular and well known for his dinosaur sculptures. This Web site is an online archive of many of Sibbick's realistic works, including *Ankylosaurus, Brachiosaurus, Triceratops,* and many more. A real pleasure to surf.

http://www.palaeo.gly.bris.ac.uk/dinobase/picturesJS/
dinopicturesJS.html

MICHAEL SKREPNICK

Working with paleontologists like Dr. Phil Currie to bring bone beds to life in artwork has been part of Michael Skrepnick's life for many years now. This Web site shares pieces of Skrepnick's art and his life experiences through written notes and visual galleries.

http://www.dinosaursinart.com

JOE TUCCIARONE

There is something almost magical about Joe Tucciarone's magnificent dinosaur paintings. He captures surprising settings, including nightscapes, with mystery and scientific precision. His paintings are like dinosaur dreams, and you can see a great group of his images on this easy-to-navigate Web site.

http://members.aol.com/dinoplanet/dinosaur.html

DAN VARNER

Click on Dan Varner's Web site and you'll be greeted by the jaws of prehistoric monsters. But these marine reptiles weren't imaginary. They were real, and Dan captures their ferocity and wonder. A great chance to look back in time—and deep into the Late Cretaceous waters!

http://www.oceansofkansas.com/varner.html

ROBERT WALTERS

Few are the dinosaur experts who haven't heard of Bob Walters. His attention to accuracy and fine detail are legendary. On this beautiful Web site, you'll see his work in stages as it moves from sketches to finished murals. You'll also see other samples of his work, his bio, and a list of publications featuring his work. A great chance to study one of the masters.

http://www.dinoart.com

DINOSAUR ART AND MODELING

Links to dozens of dinosaur resources with a focus on art and modeling. A fun way to explore many artists from one clearinghouse Web site.

http://www.indyrad.iupui.edu/public/jrafert/dinoart.html

DINOSAUR ILLUSTRATIONS, IN GENERAL

This is a great no-frills list of dinosaur artwork, from nostalgic to playful to scientifically accurate. Don't expect bells and whistles. Instead, expect rows and rows of links to dinosaur art pieces.

http://www.search4dinosaurs.com

PUBLICATIONS

FOSSIL NEWS

Called the journal for "avocational" paleontology, this collection of articles, artwork, and research opportunities edited by Lynne Clos is designed for the fossil fan with a little more paleontological background than the average person. It's of interest to professionals, of course. But it's geared toward non-professionals, and successfully so. A terrific resource.

http://www.fossilnews.com

GEOSCIENCE BOOKS

If you're in the market for a rare or out-of-print book focused on the geological sciences, look no more. If it's humanly possible, GeoScience Books should have it—or at least know where to look.

http://www.geosciencebooks.com

JOURNAL OF DINOSAUR PALEONTOLOGY

Jeff Poling is a remarkable guy. For more than fifteen years, he's been an online font of knowledge when it comes to dinosaurs and the science that studies them. In this very user-friendly collection of articles, Poling makes it possible for fossil fans to easily catch up on dinosaur news—recent and/or not so recent. Click on the live-link headlines and you'll be transported to the articles. This is a Web site you'll find yourself revisiting again and again.

http://www.dinosauria.com/jdp/jdp.htm

PALEOPUBLICATIONS

Like GeoScience Books, if you're looking for an out-of-print or antique paleontology book or publication, you've found the resource of your dreams in

PaleoPublications. A great chance to stock up on what came before—to better understand what's new and in the news.

http://www.paleopubs.com

PREHISTORICS ILLUSTRATED

If you are a fan of dinosaur artwork—new, old, famous, obscure—you'll want to make Prehistorics Illustrated one of your browser's "favorite places," because it is a pure gold mine! One of my favorite features is the alphabetized dinosaur general list—a resource that lists dinosaur names and various artistic representations of that dinosaur via user-friendly links. There is so much here, you might not know where to start. An amazing cyber-library of dinosaur and other prehistoric images.

http://www.prehistoricsillustrated.com

PREHISTORIC TIMES

Six times a year, editor Mike Fredericks publishes the *Prehistoric Times* from his office in Folsom, California. The striking covers alone are more than worth the subscription price. But don't miss a word inside. From interviews to illustrations, it's a magazine you'll want to read and keep for years to come. Serious science for dinosaur fans of every kind.

http://www.gremlins.com/prehistoric_times

SCIENCE DAILY

Paleontology isn't the only scientific discipline covered in *Science Daily,* but it is covered with journalistic integrity, just as the latest news happens. If it's cutting-edge dinosaur science you're looking for, *Science Daily* will give you the lowdown.

http://www.sciencedaily.com/news/fossils_summaries.php

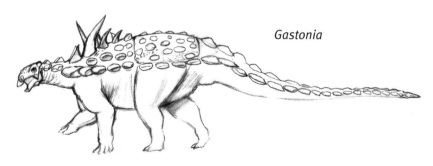

Gastonia

INTERACTIVE

BILLY BEAR LAND O' DINOSAURS ACTIVITIES

Younger kids will find numerous dinosaur-related games, crafts, study guides, and coloring pages on this popular children's Web site.

http://www.billybear4kids.com/dinosaurs/long-long-ago.html

DINOFUN DINOSAUR GAMES

Silly dinosaur-related games and puzzles are stockpiled at this Web site designed for younger fossil fans. Terrific fun for elementary school ages.

http://www.dinofun.com

DINOFUN E-MAIL POSTCARDS

If you're in a zany dinosaur mood, you won't want to miss these fun electronic dinosaur postcards you can send via e-mail. From a freaky winking *Triceratops* to an animated dancing dino, you'll find something to please your favorite paleo-pal.

http://www.dinofun.com/postoffice.html

DINOSAUR BATH

Want to plant a plastic dinosaur in soap? Look no further than this "how-to" Web site! A quirky way to celebrate your love for things dinosaurian.

http://www.meltandpour.com/dinobath.htm

DINOSAUR CLIP ART

Kids Domain offers hundreds of clip-art images in its Icon Mania collection, including a terrific set of twelve Agrapha 32-bit dinosaur icons, and much, *much* more. If you're building a dinosaur Web site, don't miss this terrific resource.

http://www.kidsdomain.com/icon/dino.html

DINOSAUR GAMES

The same online organization that brought us the dinosaur icons for Web site construction offers a group of kid-friendly dinosaur games on this branch of its Web site. Worth a wander, if you're in the mood to play.

http://www.kidsdomain.com/games/dino.html

DINOSAUR TRIVIA GAME

Answer ten Jurassic Period dinosaur trivia questions and see how well you know your ancient history!

http://www.cascoly.com/games/triv/trivprep.asp?game=dino&nq=1

DINOSAURWORLD GAMES

Lots of dinosaur word games are archived on this Web site, but the various coloring sheets are especially fun to download, print, and tackle with pencils, crayons, or paint. A nice option for educators looking for free art to share with students at school.

http://www.dinosaurworld.com/games.html

DINOWEB DINOSAUR POSTCARDS

More terrific dinosaur postcards from a European Webmaster. A bit more serious than the playful options from DinoFun, they might appeal to slightly older paleo-fans.

http://www.dino-web.com/cards.html

DINOWEB GAMES

Are you good at matching games? Labyrinths? Puzzles? Then this dinosaur-themed game site is for you! There are more than a dozen choices for kids ages nine to fourteen. Look for dot to dots, dinosaur-imposter games, shockwave animation games, and much more.

http://www.dino-web.com/games.html

DISCOVERING DINOSAURS ACTIVITY GUIDE

A vibrant dinosaur activity guide from Encyclopedia Britannica Online, complete with news updates, theory explorations, and a teacher's guide for classroom applications.

http://www.search.eb.com/dinosaurs/dinosaurs/study

HANDS-ON CRAFT FOR KIDS DINOSAUR SOAP

A different recipe for making soap, just in case the melt-and-pour method doesn't fit your dinosaur soap–making needs. Washing up is never more fun than when a dinosaur is inside the soap bar!

http://www.craftsforkids.com/projects/dinosoap.htm

KINETOSAURS

Looking for dinosaur arts and crafts? The Children's Museum of Indianapolis has put together a great selection on its colorful, user-friendly Web site. Photos and instructions are included.

http://www.childrensmuseum.org/special_exhibits/
kinetosaur/index.html

NAME THAT REPTILE

Want a dinosaur challenge? Name the reptiles—meat-eaters, flying reptiles, plant-eaters, marine reptiles, and more—on this Web site quiz arena. It's great fun for dinosaur fans of all ages.

http://www.sdnhm.org/kids/dinosaur/namegame/how2play.html

SEND A POSTCARD

Are you a fan of the old-school, pen-and-ink dinosaur illustrations that blazed the trail for today's realistic paleo-artists? Then these e-mail postcards will be a real treasure to discover. With nine different nostalgic options, these are truly wonderful old illustrations most fossil fans will admire.

http://www.search4dinosaurs.com/postcard.html

WHITE CHOCOLATE BABY DINOSAUR EGG

Ready to eat some paleo-treats? Then whip up some white chocolate dinosaur eggs—with gummy dinosaurs inside! The recipe and detailed instructions are available online at this creative Web site.

http://www.recipesource.com/desserts/candy/wc-dino-egg1.html

Ceratosaurus baby